The Dragon Slayer
Reflections on the Saving of the World

Jim McGuiggan

For
my brother
Alex
&
in warm memory
of our sister
Annie

Other Books By Jim McGuiggan

www.jimmcguiggan.com

To order the following please contact
International Biblical Resources
Billie Paine at 877-792-6408

The God Who Commands the Impossible (published 2003)
The Reign of God
The Power To See It Through
Genesis and Us

Commentaries:
The Book of Isaiah
The Book of Daniel
The Book of Romans
The Book of Revelations

Available through Howard Publishing
West Monroe, La. 800-858-4109

The God of the Towel
Jesus Hero of Thy Soul
Where the Spirit of the Lord Is
Let Me Count the Ways

Available through Waterbrook Press
A division of Random House

Celebrating the Wrath of God

Available through Covenant Publishing
Webb City, Missouri 877-673-1015

Life On the Ash Heap

TABLE OF CONTENTS

The Cross

The Crux of the Matter

"It isn't the crucifixion

that gives glory to Christ

but Christ that gives

meaning and glory

to the crucifixion"

Preaching the Cross

There were those who would apologize for the doctrine of the cross but Paul wasn't one of them. He said, "We *preach* Christ crucified"—we don't whisper it. "We preach Christ crucified," said J.H. Jowett, "we don't timidly submit it for subdued discussion in the academic grove; we don't offer it to the hands of exclusive circles—we preach it, we stand out like the town-crier in the public way, and we proclaim it to the common and indiscriminate crowd."

Lothar Coenen (*New International Dictionary New Testament Theology, 3.48-57*) reminds us that in classical times, the kerux (the preacher), was the person who was commissioned by his ruler or the state to call out some item of news to the public with a distinct, clear voice. Despite some differences in function and self-understanding, that's what the early church did. They stood out in public and with loud voices so that everyone could hear they preached about a crucified Christ and thought they were saving the world (1 Corinthians 1:21)!

The Cross and Our Changed Lives

"We preach *Christ* crucified" he said—we don't preach our own commitment or holy lives. In 2 Corinthians 4:5, in the face of those who loved the limelight, he said "we proclaim not ourselves; we proclaim Christ Jesus as Lord." And why not, since *he* is the Lord and Savior! Our changed lives are no substitute for the atoning life and death of Jesus Christ so we mustn't offer our moral and spiritual attainment as a *necessary* proof of the cross. It isn't our transformed lives that make the cross the moral and spiritual center of the universe. It's the cross that creates our transformed lives as a witness to the true moral and spiritual center of the universe—Jesus Christ and him crucified.

But we shouldn't hesitate to thank God for and speak of the way he has changed our lives. These are a part of the proof of the truth of the gospel because they make Christ's cosmic victory concrete in local places. But they can't stand alone and they mustn't be made a substitute for or a mask that hides the cross events themselves. What transforms us and shapes our lives is the cross. In a very real sense our lives don't validate the gospel but the gospel makes sense of our lives. It's true that we need more than words about the cross if we're to make the whole gospel known all around us. Along with the message and Bible study we must have discipleship and outreach because this too is an aspect of the redeeming work of Christ. But it is the Christ himself that we speak and sing and pray and live. If we hide him behind our fine lives and gentle ways and lovely marriages and families we are obscuring the gospel by which the world and we are saved.

"We preach *Christ* crucified"—we don't preach the crucifixion of Christ. It isn't the crucifixion that gives glory to Christ but Christ that gives meaning and glory to the crucifixion. It isn't a deed we proclaim but a person who embraced and accomplished the deed we call the crucifixion. It isn't the bare act of dying we proclaim but the person who accomplished the dying. It isn't the bare act of dying we proclaim but the meaning and purpose and effects of that act of dying.

Nevertheless, it is Christ *crucified* that we preach. While in John 10:18 Jesus insisted that no one robbed him of his life and that he chose to follow the will of his Father by laying it down, he was still seized and killed.

This was no death of old age or "natural causes". It would be a tragedy to underestimate how much is revealed in the incarnation but it would also be a calamity to short-circuit the meaning of the incarnation by avoiding the cross. Luther raged against the theologians of glory who wanted all the sweetness and light of logic but exorcised the cross. To reject the cross as the critical point of the revelation and work of God is to create a god in our own image. Whatever else the cross says, it says that God will not be boxed-in, he will reveal himself as he is and not as we determine he can or cannot be.

The united witness of the whole biblical corpus is to be given its place but the cross is the peak from which everything is to be surveyed and understood.

The crucifixion wasn't merely a *way* of dying it was a *kind* of dying; it was a violent death at the hands of transgressors. It was humanity conspiring to do away with the unique Son of God and by doing so revealing unfathomed depths to our sin. On the other hand it was the supreme act of obedience in the life of a holy Son that crowned and completed his self-offering to his Holy Father as humanity's redeeming representative (Philippians 2:8).

His death was more than something he and his Father agreed would take place, it was a purposed attack on the satanic kingdom. Revelation 12:11 in an outburst of joyful praise tells us the followers of Christ overcame Satan "by the blood of the Lamb". Not by his pitying love, not by his warm affection, not by his tolerance and bravery, not by his sweet words and true teaching, but by his blood! All these other things must be taken up into that death or that death has no meaning or atoning value. But all these things must be taken up into his *death* because his death was the crowning moment of his life; it was the point at which he offered all that he was and did and meant to do on our behalf. However it is to be spelled out, the death of Christ is the judgement of God against the sin of a whole humanity. *Jesus' death was not so much his getting what we deserved, as it was the Holy Father getting what he deserved.* What Christ ceaselessly offered his Holy Father in his daily living is brought to focus in a cross that consummated his holy obedient life. In the cross we see God getting what he deserved; what we should always have given him. Finally and completely a human gave to God, as an obedient child, what the Holy Father was worthy of.

His wasn't only a death that spoke the judgement of God against sin and offered to God his holy due, it was tasted "for" (on behalf of) every person (Hebrews 2:9). It was as Scots theologian P.T. Forsyth said, *for* every person, *from* every person, *as* every person and, because he was always alone except for Him who never left him, it was *apart* from every person. He died alone in a sense in which it wasn't possible for anyone else to die alone.

We make much of his death. How could we do otherwise? We speak of its glory, its power, its love and heroism—all true but in a very real sense it was "just another death". Though we now know differently, at that time and for so many on that day the crucifixion was nothing they hadn't seen or heard of before; it was back to the daily grind once the initial hubbub died away. "He tasted the average man's death, not the hero's alone, the death of the little man, the failure and collapse of the man in a mean way of moral business, the cave-dwellers of the conscience. He tasted that in our moral death which is most universal, the commonness of it, the sorriness of it, what gives it access to all doors, and entrance at the very cracks and chinks in the rear of our nature. He tasted death from a generation of vipers. It was death by sickly candlelight in a little house in a back street among miles of them. It was death made cheap, death for the million."

But it was *that* cheap and ordinary death that the church proclaimed because for all it's ordinariness it was the most momentous event in human history.

Glory In a Public Lynching

Of all the things Paul could have boasted in who would have thought, in light of his early years, that he would ever have said this? "But no boasting for me, none, except in the cross of our Lord Jesus Christ, by which the world has been crucified to me and I crucified to the world." (Galatians 6:14, Moffatt) He'd seen and heard a lot. He'd seen many fabulous temples such as those of Artemis and Aphrodite, magnificent Greek sculpture, Roman legions and endless miles of Roman roads. He'd been to famous places like Thermopylae where 300 Spartans galvanized the Greek world into war that shook the kingdom of mighty Xerxes to fragments. He was well acquainted with Herod the Great's astonishing temples and shrines and fortresses. He had heard Greek orators, knew about the great philosophers and poets and perhaps could have been the class valedictorian under Gamaliel. He'd even been to heaven! The great Moses only went up a mountain and heard things he could repeat but Paul went into heaven itself and heard things too wonderful to repeat. He knew his heritage and the glory that had been the Maccabean era when a little army the size of a postage stamp drove Antiochus IV out of his mind, but none of that captured his imagination or sent him careering all over creation. If it had all been pieced together in one sequence and filmed in Technicolor it wouldn't have made any difference. "No boasting for me, none, *except...*"

There was an exception. Not only would he boast in that, no one could get him to stop his boasting in it. And what was it he strode half way across the world bragging about? What is it that set him on fire that he cared so little about his life that he left pints of his blood on the outskirts of every town in Asia Minor? Well? What was it?

A public lynching on a public gallows!

This Paul said he would brag on. This and nothing else! In light of the *shame* that was attached to death on a cross the irony in it is so thick you could cut it with a knife and spread it like butter on toast.

The Enduring Power of the Cross

The cross of Christ isn't an apology! And we aren't to talk about it as though we were continually apologizing. We aren't to talk about it as if we wanted people to "pity poor Jesus for what we did to him." The cross can speak for itself and has been doing that for millennia and it has been burying false gods and half-gods everywhere it was truly seen.

Heinrich Heine, German-born poet and literary figure, after quoting the Homeric description of the feasting gods, says: "Then suddenly approached, panting, a pale Jew with drops of blood on his brow, with a crown of thorns on his head, and a great cross laid on his shoulders; and he threw the cross on the high table of the gods so that the golden cups tottered, and the gods became dumb and pale, and grew even paler till at last they melted away into vapor." ("Die Stadt Lucca" (The City of Lucca) "Reisebilder, Bd. 4" (Travel Pictures, Vol. 4), 1831.)

Apologize for that?

The Challenge and Recklessness of the Cross

John Tolkein, the author of *Lord of the Rings,* didn't think much of Dorothy Sayers' writing but any believer is bloodless that isn't stirred at times by this rehearsal of the plain unvarnished facts of the faith.

> Jesus Bar-Joseph, the carpenter of Nazareth was...the God 'by whom all things were made.'...He was not a kind of demon or fairy pretending to be human; He was in every respect a genuine living man. He was not merely a man so good as to be 'like God'—He was God. Now, this is not just a pious commonplace; it is not a commonplace at all. For what it means is this...that for whatever reason God chose to make man as he is—limited and suffering and subject to sorrows and death—He had the honesty and the courage to take His own medicine...When He was a man, He played the man. He was born in poverty and died in disgrace and thought it well worth while...Possibly we might prefer not to take this tale too seriously—there are disquieting points about it. Here we had a man of Divine character walking and talking among us—and what did we do with Him?...Our leading authorities in Church and State considered that he talked too much and uttered too many disquieting truths. So we bribed one of His friends to hand Him over quietly to the police, and we tried Him on a rather vague charge of creating a disturbance, and had Him publicly flogged and hanged on the common gallows, 'thanking God we were rid of a knave.' All this is not very creditable to us, even if He was (as many people thought and think) only a harmless crazy preacher. But if the Church is right about Him, it was more discreditable still; for the man we hanged was God Almighty.

So that is the outline of the official story—the tale of the time when God was the under-dog and got beaten, when He submitted to the conditions He had laid down and became a man like the men He had made, and the men He had made broke Him and killed Him. This is the dogma we find so dull—the terrifying drama of which God is the victim and hero…

*"Now we may call that doctrine exhilarating or we may call it devastating; we may call it revelation or we may call it rubbish; but if we call it dull, then words have no meaning at all…*that man should play the tyrant over God and find Him a better man than himself is an astonishing drama indeed. Any journalist, hearing it for the first time, would recognize it as News; those who did hear it for the first time actually called it News, and good news at that; though we are apt to forget that the word Gospel ever meant anything so sensational.

Perhaps the drama is played out now, and Jesus is safely dead and buried. Perhaps. It is ironical and entertaining to consider that once at least in the world's history those words might have been spoken with complete conviction, and that was upon the eve of the Resurrection." (I added the italics.)

"Is this a miracle or what?! How is it that we can become so absorbed in the daily newspapers? How can we be glued to the twenty-four hour news stations listening to the same banal rehearsals from presenters doing their best to make it sound exciting? Sayers' mind-boggling summary is, in fact, the *reality* of our faith! Can you imagine how astonished the Christ would be if he walked in on one of our customary sermons when we verbally rape everyone outside the building (and many inside it) for every conceivable thing and call it "faithful" *gospel* preaching?

Preaching, Boredom and the Cross

It's only because we're overly familiar with Galatians 6:14 that we don't drop down on our knees sucking for breath when somebody repeats it. We can't now feel as people felt when they first heard the words. When Greeks shook their heads in grinning unbelief and Jews choked in anger over them (as many do to this day) at least the meaning of the cross was *felt* though it wasn't understood. Now we "understand" it and don't feel it. But the truth is—isn't it?—that we don't really understand it at all because we have reduced it to a sickly sweet sentimentalism in God. A God who will forgive us anything. Anything! Even our sinful boredom that yawns in the face of his eternal excitement and earnestness.

We don't do a lot of bragging on the ancient marvels or a lot of oohing and aahing over the glories of former days but we have our own categories to glory in. How far we can jog, what we can bench-press, what they think of us in the academies, how many church conferences we headline, how much our new vehicle set us back and how young everyone says we look even at our age. We like to brag on where we've backpacked to, how many celebrities we can count as our friends, how great our marriage is and how it is that our kids have never given us a moment's trouble. We're able to glory in our grasp of biblical correctness and we tell how large and devoted our congregations are.

All...good...stuff...worth...bragging...on. Nothing there to be ashamed of!

Well...not exactly.

Maybe we should be ashamed that the cross doesn't send us reeling more often. Maybe we should be ashamed that we're so socially sophisticated, having seen so much and traveled so far, that we are so blasé about the cross. Maybe the shame is that all these other lovely things eclipse the cross and bring back the Friday darkness to him. That Friday darkness in which the Master died—feeling abandoned. Maybe we should be ashamed and a little afraid that we can hear this without noting its imperial demands. Perhaps we who minister the Word should be ashamed of the fact that when someone asks us about the cross the only things we can trot out are the same well-worn one-liners rather than rich and uplifting teaching. Maybe we should be ashamed that we don't pore over it more often in search of its astonishing depths. If we really do have a gospel as rich as we say then it's no wonder that Sylvester Horne said this in his Yale Lectures on preaching:

> Some trades and professions, it is clear, will die out as the kingdom of God comes to its own. But for every voice that carries inspiration to its fellows; for every soul that has some authentic word from the Eternal wherewith to guide and bless mankind there will always be a welcome. No changes of the future can cancel the commission of the preacher…Let every village preacher who climbs into a rude rostrum, to give out a text and preach a sermon to a meager handful of somewhat stolid hearers, remember to what majestic Fraternity he belongs and what romantic tradition he inherits.

The Cross and Our Awful Need

I know we say it over and over again but it really is true. And I know it has the advantage of sounding pious but it's nevertheless true. *The cross is too vast in its meaning for anyone or all of us together to get to the bottom of it.* It'll never be the case that we'll say, "Well, that's that fully explained so let's move on to something else." You only have to dip into the literature about the cross to come away gob-smacked, shaking your head and muttering something like, "I didn't realize…" So no one pretends he or she has said all there is to be said. Even that previous sentence is so needless that it borders on a smarmy piety or the utterly banal. But it leads me to say that this little book, while it takes into account some of the rich exploration that has gone on for centuries can only offer pointers and suggestions that might lead to further pointers and suggestions. Most writers profess to do no more than that.

To see the cross as any *one* thing is not only to underestimate its glory it's also to underestimate our awful need. If the cross only brings acquittal—end of story—where are we to find holy freedom and the power that recreates us in the likeness of the Holy Father? If the cross brings us only pardon and leaves us still as impenitent rebels who hold the

Holy Father in contempt or in utter apathy who will transform us within and so reconcile us to the Father?

And if the cross supplies all the things we need (and it certainly does!) how should we *tell* the good news to the world? How will we phrase it? Understanding what God truly has done and is doing it, in and as Jesus Christ the crucified one, how will we *express* it? That's what this little book is about—it's about ways of telling what God has done and is doing for us as he unveiled (and unveils) himself in and as Jesus Christ, the crucified One.

The Drama of the Cross

Just the bare facts of the Christian story can send a thrill up your spine if they're well told. I would say even if they're not well told but we seem so dependent on the packaging these days (or was that always true?). The bare facts, rehearsed above, often left Dorothy L. Sayers thunderstruck and it peeved her that a sweet philosophy of gentle living was substituted for the dogma itself. It's true that we can be astonishingly blasé about the most profound events in ancient history or even last week and I'm not sure that that's avoidable in humans. But having said that, it's still pretty impressive that we who profess the name of Christ can chat away amiably even while someone is pouring out his or her heart about the meaning of the crucifixion from behind a pulpit or a cup of coffee.

I don't know all the reasons why that's true (of course I don't!) but I'm persuaded that we've come to see the Christian faith as another one of the competing "ways to live". We'd quickly add that it is the best one by far but I'm sure that a host of us think that the Christian faith would be just as useful and fruitful without the "dogma". The half-truth that begins, "I'd rather see a sermon than hear one any day" illustrates nicely how we expertly disembowel the gospel of Jesus Christ.

And maybe that's one of the reasons we can chat away amiably while someone is pouring out his or her heart about the crucifixion. Maybe what they're pouring out is the well-worn, one-more-time moralizings about the meaning of the cross. The cross is no longer an offence or a revelation of both God and us that makes our mouths drop open; it has become nothing more than the story of a sweet-spirited, clean-living young man who loved people and if need be was willing to die for them. "And as we leave this place let's all be like him and the world will be a better, happier place, Amen." I'm sure even the most pious among us, after a ceaseless diet of that pap, would look around for a conversation partner in or out of the church building.

And it doesn't surprise me that by the time boys or girls are fourteen years old many of them feel they've heard quite enough moralizing to last a lifetime. *Sixteen tons of bland moralizing and not an ounce of dogma, mission or destiny offered to them.* There are only so many ways we can tell each other to be nice before tedium and nausea sets in! A six-year-old, happy pagan visiting Sunday school with her friend for the first time had heard enough and wasn't afraid to voice her opinion, "This is boring!" she belted out. Her seven-year-old mentor, Lizzie, hissed at her, "Keep your voice down it's *supposed* to be boring."

The cross is about more than being "sweet"! Reducing the gospel and the Christian faith in that way dulls it and completely ignores the New Testament claims about the cross of Jesus, the son of Mary. But we're all so tolerant these days, aren't we? "Let's have less theology and dogma because this is the sort of thing that keeps believers apart. We all know how we're supposed to live so let's get on with it and leave the dogmatic questions to the ivory-tower people. Anyway, theology and dogma mean little or nothing to the man or woman in the street." Hmmm, I wonder how long it's been since the man or woman in the street was offered theology and dogma?

The Need for Serious Reflection on the Cross

Maybe it'd be a great change if we came across grease-covered mechanics arguing the case for and against Theodore Beza's hyper-Calvinism while they tried to cure a dying oil pump or palpitating carburetor. How would it strike you if the hairdresser were arguing with her customer about the strengths and weakness of Peter Abelard's atonement views rather than them trotting out one-more-time the tedious bromides about "niceness"? What if the Bible classes (and later the foyers) were bee-hives of discussion about God's sovereignty, human free will and the stunning grace of God rather than filled with contented drones that confirmed how "interesting" and "delightful" the morning sermon was? Besides, anyone who thinks that the average man and woman had nothing to do with the rise of these theological and dogmatic issues ought to think again.

Much of Paul's theology was generated because Simeon, the saddle-maker and his friends asked, "How does the Messiahship of Jesus of Nazareth fit in with the election of Israel, the place of the Torah and Yahweh's faithfulness?" The New Testament form of monotheism was developed because somebody scratched his head and asked how the Carpenter fitted into the Godhead, if at all. How could he be human if he was God and how could he be God if he was human? Though it may be true I have my doubts that the average woman and man is bored with theology and dogma; but if they are maybe it's because we've made it appear dull and irrelevant when it's neither. It just might be that people like myself have fallen under the spell of *telling* the Story rather than under the spell of the Story we're to tell. Where that's true the big issue becomes homiletics, how to communicate well, how to get and keep the listener's attention and the astonishing gospel gets lost in the grand parade of preaching brilliance. We eyeball the frame with pride and satisfaction and the picture is just so much background material. But it's the cross that saves and not the wise words well spoken! If we spent more time diving into the depths of the cross and came up breathless but with treasure galore maybe how we say it would take care of itself. Maybe then people would pack the classrooms and church-buildings. But even if they didn't....

The Cross and the Individual

There's something else I think needs saying. There's a glory about the cross and resurrection of Jesus Christ that we miss because we're so obsessed with, "What does that mean _to me?_" It's right and proper to take a personal view of life but it's a blunder of great proportions to go on and on about the individual and miss the cosmic dimensions of God's work.

With heads and hearts in the spiritual trough, ducking for personal goodies, we reduce the cosmic to the individual, not knowing that to miss the cosmic is to miss the glory involved in the personal. We link vast galactic truths to an agenda that is too personal and we end up with a bull elephant pulling a three-inch Tinker Toy. Some believers even dare to implore God to get them a hairdresser who can fix their hair the way they want it (yes!). God has redeemed a whole creation, it groans in eager expectation longing for the day when the children of God are revealed in inexpressible glory. We're obsessed with hair-dos and convenient parking places?!

However it distresses our little hearts to be reminded that we're only one of countless millions God created to enrich and glorify. But we mustn't feed our hunger for personal "spiritual intimacy" and "wooing" by robbing God of the glory of his vision and the vastness of his heart. "For God so loved _the world!_"

The Claims and Drift of This Little Book

This book takes it as true that Satan and humans joined together in rebellion against God and built a world of their own. Not a literal, physical world you understand, for neither Satan nor a human can create a single blade of grass or a molecule of spit. No, the world they created and create is a sinful and mental reconstruction of the world that *God* created. In truth, it isn't really a world so much as it is a powerful worldview. When they were done they perverted, abused and worshipped all things God had made (including themselves) and they excluded him from their deformed and cheap world (not that he could want any part of it though he's in sovereign control of it).

Since it was sinful Satan's idea and the humans went along with it Satan was declared the prince of it and everyone followed his malevolent lead. It wasn't that he *owned* them (how could he? he was a sinner like them; nothing more, just a fellow-sinner), it was that they became like him and spread the infectious treachery and cynicism they'd learned from him. The humans were no mindless pawns, you understand. They chose to make his agenda their own and every new generation of sinners grins and goes along with his infernal majesty. Well, they don't always grin and in fact before they're old enough to think about it they're biased in favor of the satanic agenda and they spiral downward as the years pass. So there is in the human experience that blend of victim and rebel status and part of the human crime is that it won't acknowledge its dire need and awful sin.

This little book says that out of love God created and purposed to bring that creation from glory to glory even though it meant his being faithful in the face of humanity's abysmal lack of faithfulness. But because that glory could only be fulfilled to humans who were in holy fellowship with him God moved to redeem them from the sin. It was sin that not only *created* a rupture in their relationship with him but also *was* the rupture. Sin had to be *atoned,* that is, so dealt with that it would be neutralized. So that reconciliation could take place and the glorious finale could be experienced. This book rehearses the gospel how that God came in and as Jesus Christ to be part of Adam's sinful family. He did this so that in its name and for its sake he would resist "the world" and give to God the holy homage due him. Being one of Adam's sinful family he shared with it God's holy and redemptive judgement on its sin. He confessed as a man, that in this redemptive judgement God was righteous. But because Jesus was *God* being a man and because he was bearing his own judgement against sin Jesus shows God righteousness is not mere retributive justice, it is *faithfulness* to his commitment to the human family and his creation at large.

This book insists that at the *individual and personal level* sin is not atoned for if a sinner continues to cherish and live in sin as an expression of his or her rejection of God. What Christ has done with sin must be made our own by faith. The book also insists that that personal appropriation of the cross of Christ is God's work and not ours; it is not self-generated, self-reflective or self-sustaining.

The book also claims that the atoning work of Christ confirms and brings to fulfillment God's glorious plans for the whole of creation. The resurrection of Christ is the beginning of a new humanity. The new humanity; a new way of being a human and exercising dominion over a creation redeemed from the curse. He is the first and the firstborn of all who will be raised to immortality and when humans experience in fact, as individuals, what Christ has already experienced as an individual, they will be glorified and immortal humans. When that occurs, the whole creation will be delivered from its bondage into a surpassing glory.

You might find something here that will whet your appetite for something richer and more demanding so why don't you give this little book a good read and move on to better material. There is some degree of repetition and overlap in some sections (you'll know it when you meet it) but it's mostly deliberate because there are so many rich little nuances to complex truth. Some of you who are well read and experienced might be a little put off by the repetition. ("How many times does he need to say the same thing?") On the other hand, I don't think it's *mere* repetition.

For all those who think the only good book is one that "moves" you or makes you "soar" this little thing will be a bitter disappointment. But it might be a good little book for all that.

I'm open to criticism on any proposal I've made here so feel free to sound off.

jim mcguiggan

holywoodjk@aol.com

The Road Leading to Bethlehem and Golgotha

"…. what unites God and us as men is that He does not will to be God without us…"

God Moved Against Sin

Whatever else is unclear in scripture this much is clear: God in Jesus Christ has moved against Sin. I won't stop at this point to cite texts because the claim is so transparently true as not to need proof. The cross of Christ says that sin troubles God and should trouble us.

Why Did God Move Against Our Sin?

The Swiss theologian, Karl Barth, a prophetic figure kicked out of Germany by the Nazis, thought the answer was unfathomable and yet simple. He said (Church Dogmatics, 4.1, page 7): "To put it in the simplest way, what unites God and us as men is that He does not will to be God without us...He does not allow His history to be His and ours ours..." He does not will to be God without us! How many truths have you heard more profound than that?

And F.W. Faber offered his own often quoted explanation for God's astonishing move against our sin when he said:

God loves to be longed for
He longs to be sought
For he sought us himself with such longing and love
He died for desire of us
Marvelous thought
And he longs for us now to be with him above.

The way some of us talk you'd think there was only one reason God moved against our sin—he got mad. I wonder why it is that that is the first thing we think? (List your reasons sometime and I'll list mine.) Imagine a godly and loving father. Imagine a much-loved child who insults the father and heads out and begins a downward spiral. The father leaps into action to deal with the child's "sin" and predicament. What's in his mind? He feels the insult and takes the boy's contempt of the "house rules" seriously? I wouldn't doubt it, but is that the thing he first thinks of? God must take his holiness and his law seriously but is the thought that these have been violated the first and dominant driving force that move him against our sin? Certainly they'd have to be part of a comprehensive answer but what's wrong with imagining that he jumps to his feet prepared to do what his holy love requires to save his beloved children? Why can't his anger be part of a more comprehensive motivation rather than the overwhelming and central thrust of atonement?

Our Need and God's Agenda

Why did God move against Sin? I suppose his nature and character and his love for us would help us to determine that. Whatever else "sin" is, it is relational infidelity--first and foremost it is against God himself. There's no doubt that he sees sin as an insult to his majesty, contempt of his holiness and rebellion against his Lordship. Yes, and what else? He sees it as ingratitude in the face of his generosity, arrogance instead of humility and treachery instead of glad-hearted allegiance. And what else? He sees it as blind pride and a claim to godlike independence. We say things like this to keep from saying nothing. But we know that in the eyes of God, sin is the one unendurable (he says so!). Sin is a reality he cannot, *will* not live at peace with under any circumstances.

But there's another face of Sin that moves God to deal with it. He also sees it as a power that destroys his beloved, enslaves his children and cheats them out of the fullness of life he longs to bless them with. And it deprives him of the joy he finds in their love for him. God is not only holy, he is a holy lover and that too is what moves him against Sin. There will be more than one reason that he moves to destroy Sin so we should expect to find them expressed as we go through scripture.

Because he is light and cannot fellowship moral darkness he must find a way to bring his wayward beloved into the light. He cannot do other than to take his own holiness seriously for that sets the parameters within which life with him must be lived. It isn't that he is super-sensitive about his reputation or that he will sulk if we don't treat him as we "ought" to treat him. It's because he is holy and chooses to be holy that the only life he can offer is life that has loving holiness at the heart of it.

Those who would rejoice in life with him must be holy because he is holy. He who would love and live with God will have to settle for the only God there is and he is holy! So God's call for holiness in his beloved isn't an arbitrary "condition to be met" or a hoop they must jump through to get to God. It isn't that God says, "Let's see how badly they want life. I will place this requirement before them as a 'condition of entrance'." It simply *cannot be* that those who cherish contempt of God can have life with him. It's not the fact that God prizes his honor (though Malachi 1:14 makes it very clear that he does). We might speculate that he could prize his honor in such a manner that he would immediately obliterate us when we sin, but that isn't an option for the holy God because he is a holy lover who has committed to his creation.

That being true we shouldn't be surprised to find texts that deal with atonement from the angle of God's relentless love for his wayward children. That being true we shouldn't be surprised to find God's wrath against sin and his redeeming mercy coming together in the *whole* gospel.

Difficulties and endless, needless tensions arise when we compartmentalize "qualities" or "attributes" in God. Isolate his holiness and a sinner cannot live at all. Isolate his love and we're left with a love that has no reason to deal with sin. Allow him to be, what in Christ he shows us he is, and we will find the healthy tensions in the biography of God that we find in a holy and loving earthly parent.

Two things are true of God when he moves to meet sin. *He sets himself against sin* and consequently he must deal with the sinner in whom sin exercises power. And like a good surgeon he sets himself against the sin *because he wants to redeem the sinner.* The sin that God redeems each one of us from does not exist outside of us, as though it were floating above our heads. Nor is it simply "guilt" that is wiped away. Sin becomes part of us; it shapes us, infects us, pollutes and paralyzes us. What God brings to us is more than a "status" before him ("not guilty!" or "forgiven!"); it's a dynamic mutual relationship he offers, anything less than that is less than *life.* A surgeon doesn't operate on the table on which the patient is lying precisely because the cancer or infection is *in* the patient so it's the patient that gets the knife. The surgeon isn't dealing with "disease in principle" (though that notion would be in and around the situation). He is dealing with actual disease in an actual person and so it is with God and the sinner. He makes the move to honor himself but as the scriptures insist, he honors himself by redeeming the sinner whom he loves.

God's Agenda Determines the Means by Which He Fulfills It

Knowing God in holy fellowship is life (John 17:3) and it is nothing less than life that God wants to give us. Being at one with him is not a legal matter! It is relational through and through. It is God's wayward children (see Acts 17:26-29) reconciled to him and brought to glory. Since it is not a legal matter the atoning process is not a legal process! It is all about bringing hearts and lives together. This means that in dealing with sin (atoning for sin) the crucified Christ affects how God and his wayward children relate to each other. The cross not only affects God and satisfies his holy heart it affects our unholy heart so that we find God satisfying and we are at one with him.

We can debate until the cows come home precisely how the crucified Christ functions in bringing us back to God. There can be no disputing that the New Testament teaches that that is how God brought us back to himself. Too many texts link our forgiveness and life with the blood of Christ so that connection is not open to debate.

If there is sin and it needs to be forgiven then it follows that such a forgiveness must be a righteous forgiveness; it cannot be an immoral forgiveness (compare 1 John 1:9). God cannot sin in forgiving sin.

It is in Christ that we have redemption through his blood, even the forgiveness of sins (Ephesians 1:7). If, before God, there is truly something to forgive and if in forgiving it he must be righteous as well as faithful, then the death of Christ must be the means that brings about a righteous forgiveness (1 John 1:7,9). We might speculate if God could have accomplished his purposes another way but the fact is that he didn't do it another way.

In light of his own holy love and knowing our needs, God set Jesus forth as an atoning sacrifice for our sins (Romans 3:21-26). So whatever else is true, his holy hatred of sin must be infinite and our need must have been desperate beyond measure because the cross of Christ and all it stands for is the measure of our need and God's holy love.

Dealing with our sin was not an end in itself! It was a means to an end. The end was and is nothing less than the reconciliation of the entire creation to God, that there might be a glorious new heaven and new earth in which dwells righteousness. And how did God go about accomplishing all this? He did and does it in the Christ.

God's Atoning Work in Christ Embraces Our Whole Existence

It wasn't just our "souls" that got separated from God, it was the entire person. So the atonement deals with us in our entirety. Furthermore, in dealing with sin, it is Sin God is dealing with and not just one or two of the fruits of sin. God doesn't just "happen" to be holy, he is holy because he chooses to be holy. A block of ice doesn't choose to be cold but the holy God keeps faith with himself by living out that holiness. In light of that holiness he has determined that sin has consequences and those consequences are far-reaching. God moves to deal with sin so that a whole series of interconnected realities might be created and recreated.

Specific words in scripture should be allowed to speak their peculiar truth. To use the word "saved" and pretend it tells the whole story is to cheapen our experience. To make "saved" the equivalent to "justified" is to devalue biblical currency. To say that "reconciled" is the same as "redeemed" narrows our sense of the wondrous grace God has extended to us. It's important for us to use words well so that we can speak accurately but to think and speak well will also reveal the richness of our blessings under God and in Jesus Christ.

In our discussion, to "atone" sin is to so deal with it that it no longer disrupts our relationship with God. To atone for sin is to so deal with it that it will not create a rupture if one does not already exist. In the Old Testament sacrificial arrangement the atoning sacrifices maintained Israel's relationship with God. It helps us to have a clearer picture of what God has brought and is bringing about when we know the meaning of the atonement words used (of course!). But like all words, they occur in settings that are larger than the words themselves. Lexical work helps but it isn't enough.

To propitiate or expiate, to redeem or cover and the like, certainly point the direction we should be going. But propitiate in what way? Satisfy what? Expiate how? Redeem in what respect and cover on what principle? Many of us use these terms as if they were self-explanatory and they aren't. We talk about life with God and forgiveness of sins as if they were as natural as breathing but they're no such thing. Vincent Taylor would often talk about "the astounding grace of God in Christ." With great intensity he said, "Far from being an easy assumption, fellowship with God is a desperate challenge to thought and belief." And B.F. Westcott insisted that on the surface, forgiveness of sins appears simple and easy but on a closer look, there is nothing more mysterious and more difficult. The Eastern doctrine of karma is the ever-present proof that half the world believes that true forgiveness is impossible because it despises justice. Only in our sheer ignorance do we speak as though everything was or is crystal clear. It's too profoundly and richly complex for that.

To atone for sin is to so deal with sin that the sinner may enjoy life in and with God. To atone for sin is to so deal with it that the sinner's status as sinner can be ignored without any loss of holy righteousness on God's part. The phrase "life in and with God" will do as a working description of what God wants for us in and through the person and work of Jesus Christ. But the biblical development of what God wants for us is presented in many different ways and images and from many angles.

Suppose we summarize our needs like this. If we're dead we need to be made alive. If oppressive powers are lording it over us we need to be rescued from them. If we're enslaved by sin we need to be ransomed. If we're blind we need sight and if we're poor we need to be made rich. If we're overworked and burdened we need to be given ease and rest. If we're alienated in our minds we need to be reconciled to God in our minds. If we're at war with God we need to be brought into peace with God. If we're darkness because that's where we choose to live we need to be made light and drawn to live in the light. If we're in debt and unable to pay we need someone to meet that debt for us. If we're disobedient we need to be disciplined. If we are guilty we need to be acquitted. If we're unrighteous we need to be made righteous. If we're "wise," pride-filled and arrogant, we need to be humbled. If we're away from home we need to be brought home. If we're under the dominion of Sin we need to be brought into the kingdom of God. If we're born into a creation about which there is something wild, chaotic and sin-nurturing then we need it to be reconciled to God. If we're plagued by illness and hounded by death we need to be healed and made alive. In short, all that God intended and intends for us is what we need.

And all these needs exist because sin has made its power and presence felt in the human race that is loved by a Holy Father. Sin is more than a countless number of individual wrongs—it's a power that twists and cripples us; it's a power that corrupts and cheapens. It is a thick shroud of moral smog and pollution that chokes and suffocates as it corrupts. And it is *that,* that Jesus came to atone. It is *that,* that Jesus came to destroy. Sin is not only the cause of the rupture between God and us, it *is* the rupture.

So, why did God move against sin? To obliterate the sinful creation was not an option for him but to good-naturedly dismiss sin as nothing was no option either. Therefore he moved to atone sin (that is, so deal with it that it could be neutralized) to reconcile us to himself by the redemption that is gained for us in and through Jesus Christ. The mystery and challenge of the atonement and reconciliation is mysterious and challenging precisely because an infinitely holy God loves an abysmally sinful human family.

Enter the Dragon Slayer

*"God saw us pining away in
our awful state and in holy
love came to us in and as
the person, Jesus Christ."*

Beauty and the Beast

Everything about the Dragon Slayer spells the doom and despair of the Dragon. He's handsome rather than ugly, honorable rather than sly, pure rather than unclean. He's cheerful and generous while the Dragon is gloomy and grasping; he's brave, even gallant while the Dragon's gutless down to his finely manicured talons. The Dragon Slayer loves people and explodes with righteous anger at the sights and sounds of oppression whereas the Dragon hunts and feeds on the humans he thinks are vermin. The Dragon Slayer is life— the Dragon is death. The Dragon Slayer is hope— the Dragon is despair. The Dragon Slayer's a gift— the Dragon's a thief. The Dragon Slayer is light— the Dragon is darkness. The Dragon Slayer's genuine— the Dragon's a fraud. The Dragon Slayer is honor— the Dragon is treachery and betrayal. The Dragon Slayer's young and alive—the Dragon's old and decrepit.

In the biblical record Satan is the original seducer, liar and murderer (see 2 Corinthians 11:3; John 8:44 and 1 John 3:8,12 with Genesis 3 & 4). We adopted his ways and sin spread through the human family like fire in a paint factory, bringing down the whole creation with us. Night shrouded us and like lunatics we drank from Satan's cup, ate his food, dreamed his dreams and gave ourselves as the instruments of the devastation he longed to bring. In lucid moments we saw ourselves for what we had become and weary and heartsick we wished for deliverance even while we loved our chains. Our sin was not a *legal* matter; it was relational because we had sinned against a personal God, our Holy Father. And God saw us pining away in our awful state and in holy love came to us in and as the person Jesus Christ. At last we had a champion who was in our midst as one of us. God didn't merely send a book or a message or a hint or "enough evidence" for us to guess that he was for us. He came! He himself came!

No wonder the angels of the Lord told the shepherds, "Be not afraid!" What they had to tell was nothing but "glad tidings of great joy, which shall be to all people." This was the announcement not only of a message; some *one* had come to save! It was an announcement that someone had come, not *merely* to advise or teach or lead or pity (though all that is true enough). A *Savior* had arrived! No wonder Dwight and Adam.

O holy night
The stars are brightly shining
Long lay the world in sin and error pining
Then he appeared and the soul felt its worth.
A thrill of hope
The weary world rejoices
For yonder breaks a new and glorious morn
Fall on your knees
O hear the angel voices
O night divine
O night when Christ was born.

"Long" lay the world in sin and error. Not for an hour or a week or a year. Long centuries they lay "pining". Unable to hope, having no right to hope when the sin around and within them was a killer of hope. "Wishing," maybe. And then it happened. A thrill of hope, a weary, heartsick world rejoices when the sun rises to herald a glorious new morning. When a congregation sings this hymn, just listen to how the phrase "fall on your knees" comes sweeping in with an awesome power mixed with a gratitude that just won't be suppressed. "Fear not, for I bring you good tidings of great joy!" said the angel to the shepherds. Great joyful news that creates joy and it's for everyone! The wished for, longed for, and long-promised Dragon Slayer had finally come.

The Stranger That Came to Town

In chapter 1, John tells us that "he was in the world and the world was made by him and the world knew him not and he came to his own and his own received him not." Later in that chapter the Baptist said, "There is one standing among you that you don't know and I'm not worthy to tie his shoes." I wonder, did they glance around, give the young carpenter a passing glance and move on to someone more likely? It was only later that they looked him full in the face, but even then, they still didn't know who he was.

Wasn't it Lord Byron who said, "If ever God was man or man was God Jesus Christ was both"? Love that way of putting it! Maybe we can't grasp it very well and maybe after we've said all the wise things we can say about it that we know that there's more to be said. But the New Testament lays that truth out before us without apology.

The "two natures" of Jesus Christ has always been difficult for us. It would be easier to talk about Christ if he were only a man being a man. If we could say that he was such a fine young man (the finest!) that God "adopted" him as his special son (the best of the best of us); someone who reflected God better than anyone else. It would be easier to explain our Christ if this were all he was. Or would it? Maybe if we could believe that God created this unique being at some point before creation and that this creature became the one we know as Jesus Christ. Some of us thought that would make it easier. And so on. Some views of the nature and person of Jesus Christ are more easily stated and grasped until you take a closer look at the New Testament. That's when the difficulties begin to emerge.

Jesus Is God Being Man

Jesus is not an *angel* being a man! He is not God's "supreme creation" being a man, however exalted that creature might be thought to be. Jesus is not simply a man being a man however pure and majestic we know him to be. Jesus is nothing less than *God* being a man.

Specific texts can and should be looked at (of course!) but what Byron said comes from more than individual texts here and there. It comes from the grand drift of the whole Bible that comes to its grand focus in the New Testament. Both testaments are the two acts of a single drama. The Old Testament gives the New Testament its essential grounding and the New Testament gives the Old Testament what it always pointed to: the redeeming God being faithful to his commitment to his wayward creation and coming to its rescue.

Jesus Christ is God being a man. It is a continuously chosen experience on God's part. It's true that there was a point in time when he *became* a man (John 1:14 and Philippians 2:6-7) but it's also true that his incarnate state is an ongoing experience he wills to have. He became a human because he chose to and he continues to be that human because that continues to be what pleases him. As the whole creation continues to hold together by an act of God's glad choosing (see Hebrews 1:3 and Colossians 1:17), so it is with the incarnation. So when we look at Jesus Christ we not only see the one in whom God *became* a human, he is God *being* a human.

Jesus is not an angel or a phantom or a god-man or a "sort of" man. He was fully and completely a man. Jesus is God being *a man*--nothing less and nothing more. Jesus is not God being just any man, he is God being Jesus and no other man.

In the *incarnate* state he is not God being God! Prior to his incarnation he was God being God; he was God being what he has always been but when he became incarnate, he was God being a *man*, God being something he was not.

Peter is a man being a man because he was nothing more than a man. Jesus was not a man being a man; he was *God* being a man. The difference between this human and every other human is not in the quality or completeness of their mutual humanity. The difference is that they were *humans* being humans and he was *God* being a human. When we stuck a spear into his heart it was a human heart we pierced. It was fully human feet and hands and head we gouged. What Thomas saw and gladly worshiped was God being an abused and triumphant human.

An electron microscope wouldn't have shown divine *and* human blood corpuscles or genes that were half-and-half. Jesus wasn't a hybrid (a "god-man") made of two substances, for that's neither God nor man. He was always and unceasingly God being a human. He is God *and* man in the sense that he is always God always being a man but he isn't a "mix". He isn't God attached to a human and nor he is a "composite" of God and humanity as if he entered some kind of metaphysical blender. The man you saw when you saw Jesus was wholly and completely and only a man but he was *God* being that specific human.

This means that when Jesus spoke it was always a man that spoke because it was always a man that God was being. It isn't the case that in one breath a man was speaking and in the next God was speaking. Jesus was always simply a man. God was not *pretending* to be a man nor was he "most of the time" being a man. In Jesus Christ God was truly being a man and truly being a man *all* the time. Jesus was a man approved of God by miracles and signs and wonders that people saw (Acts 2:22 and 10:38) and the power he exercised was given to him.

Jesus Is God Being a Son of Adam

But being a "man" is more than having the blood and bones that a human has. When the New Testament teaches us that God became a man we're not to suppose that God borrowed a body and "used" it. God doesn't "play" Jesus the way we would play a piano. Jesus isn't a mindless puppet operated by a divine puppeteer! Jesus is a willing, choosing human and every thought and deed of his was freely chosen in his purpose to glorify his Holy Father.

It's certainly true that in Jesus, God is glorifying himself but we mustn't hide or ignore even for a moment that the glory God received was *offered* to him in this person we know as Jesus Christ. It isn't *God* believing in himself or trusting in himself or obeying himself. It is a young man, a genuine human, *one of us* that gave to God holy obedience in joy-filled love.

Nor are we supposed to think that God took on some kind of "neutral" flesh (see Hebrews 2:10-18 and 4:14-16). There is no such thing as "neutral" humanity. While it is certainly true that Jesus is the son of the virgin Mary by the quickening power of the Holy Spirit he was nevertheless a son of Adam (Luke 3:21,38) and he was made in the likeness of sinful flesh (Romans 8:3). Paul isn't saying that physical substance itself became sinful or that the genes or somatic cells of a human body become essentially anti-God. There is nothing Gnostic about the biblical teaching. But Paul does teach that sin as a power and a presence expressed itself there in embodied humans and the proof that it reigned there is seen in our sinful lives and in the fact of our deaths (see Romans 6 & 7).

Since the human family does not and can not exist as a mass of independent and free-standing units we don't sin as free-standing units. We're a single inter-dependent human family that creates and shapes its children in its own sinful image. An alien observer would look at us and know that whatever else dwells in us as a race, sin does. Our sin is a single narrative because it is the outpouring of a single family. Sin is not an "illness" that some of us have contracted while others of us look on. No, sin is a human affliction, so to speak.

Into that single sinful family came Jesus Christ and took upon him the human nature that had been the reigning center of sin for millennia. And while in flesh he condemned sin in that flesh (Romans 8:3). But it was more than that. It wasn't only "while in" that flesh he condemned sin—it was *through* that flesh, through that human nature that he damned sin. For as by a man, sin and death entered, so by a man forgiveness and life came (Romans 5:12-21). It wasn't a "special" flesh he took. Christ took the human nature that sin had gained control over; the human nature that, *because it functioned as sin's base of attack against God*, was under God's condemnation. And in that very flesh he damned sin. Such a redemption could not have been wrought from "outside". Sin can't be destroyed by a mere exercise of divine fiat! Sin can only be destroyed by holiness. Sin can only be destroyed in its citadel by holiness and that's why God became incarnate. And as Adam in his sin let loose a destructive and defiling power by his disobedience so Jesus let loose a redeeming and uplifting power by his holy obedience.

Human nature (that is, life lived out as a human) was so skewed and dominated by sin that it could not be the vehicle in or medium through which God could be fully glorified. But rather than jettison it, God became part of it and redeemed it. The creation that was dragged into the war by man's rebellion was under the curse and in need of redemption and reconciliation.

Being a "man" means that we're a part of a human society with structures already in place. We're born into an already established political, economic, social, religious (or non-religious), or other environment. Because these structures are part of a fallen establishment they share in that fallenness (the Jewish temple and Roman taxes would illustrate). They help promote the evil of the age. Into this God came and was a man who had to come to terms with all that.

Rather than jettison human society God became part of it (Colossians 1:15) and reconciled it to himself in Jesus Christ (Colossians 1:19-20) who is the new and last Adam, the second man (1 Corinthians 15:45-47). Dominion has been restored to the "new human" in whose eyes the creation is seen for what it was meant to be, a place to be rejoiced in and shaped and governed to the glory of the God.

Why Bother With All of This?

But why does this matter? Is it worth the effort to get something of a grasp on all this? Should we not just pass the subject by and spend our time imitating the sweet young carpenter who taught us all to be loving and kind? I think not. My own impression is that more than ever we need a rich, biblical and theological development and proclamation of the central truths about the God who has come to us in and as Jesus Christ. The Godhood of Jesus Christ must not be allowed to drown the truth and reality of his humanity and that genuine humanity must be seen as the human life of God.

Hymn writer and poet, F.W. Faber gave us strong and sound counsel when he wrote:

> Workman of God! Oh, lose not heart,
> *But learn what God is like;*
> And in the darkest battle-field
> Thou shalt know where to strike.

To know to some marked degree about the nature and person of Jesus Christ is to know about his work. It will open our eyes to the nature and character of God, his holiness, his relentless love and ceaseless affection for his creation. It will open our eyes to the nature of sin and the atonement. It will teach us where best to strike when we meet the enemies and it will give us the necessary tools to dismantle forts of blind folly and error that stand in God's way (2 Corinthians 10:4-6).

It matters profoundly that the young man dying on the cross is God bearing his own redemptive judgement and the sin of the world. It matters that the love and holiness seen there is *God's* love and holiness. We don't have a lovely young man telling us that he adores us and is more than willing to die for us—it's more than that. We have God in and as that young man telling it to us on the cross. This is God making himself known, not from outside the creation but from within it and as part of it. *Who Jesus is, is the revelation of what he is about!*

He is truly "God with us"! Not "with" us in the sense that raw divinity merely stands alongside us but that "raw divinity" became one of us (John 1:1-2,14) and wasn't ashamed to be called our brother (Hebrews 2:11)!

That it is *God* being the young man dying there on the tree says that the profoundest religious truth isn't about decent humanity reaching up to be near God but God coming down to be with sinful humanity. This isn't the unveiling of man (though it is the revelation of what God means man to be and what he will bring man to), it's the unveiling of God, showing himself as a human. It isn't God revealing his uncreated "essence" or "substance" (what he's "made of," so to speak); it's God revealing his nature and character *and* what that means in relation to his creation.

That it was a genuine son of Adam that defeated the Dragon is of profound encouragement to us. We know God can beat Satan but with the aid of the Holy Spirit and God's sustaining grace one of *us* beat him! And he did it in our name, praise God.

It's about something bigger than "saying things correctly" and "being nice". It's about cosmic chaos, tottering worlds and buckling empires, and about God raising humanity from the debris into the image of Christ to reign with him in holy living glory over a liberated creation (Romans 8:18-21,29-30). This is no debate about mere words but about eternal realities and if we can't see that, it's our loss and not to our credit. Maybe we can't grasp it all (of course we can't!), but to be certain that such reflection is no "waste of time" but rather a "royal waste of time" (Marva Dawn in another context) is something wonderful to be sure of.

It's true that Jesus is revealing God but it's a larger truth that Jesus is God revealing himself in and as a human. We're supposed to say, "What we're seeing and hearing here is *God* revealing himself." Less than God is not enough and more than God isn't possible. There have been tens of thousands of men and women who have shown us how to be lovely and redemptive but there is only one Jesus Christ who is altogether lovely and uniquely redemptive.

That Jesus is God being a man has profound ramifications for any doctrine of the atonement. The truth that Jesus is God incarnate buries all theories that speak as if, in his atoning work, Jesus was saving us from a God who was more than eager to damn us without chance of reprieve. The feeling still lingers in the minds of many that Jesus loves us and the Holy Father only loves us because Jesus loves us. Aside from the fact that it drives a wedge between the Father and the Son it is sheer nonsense in light of actual texts (John 3:16).

Jesus Is the One True God Unveiled

What manner of God is it that reveals himself in and as the man Jesus Christ? It's no impersonal force, no immovable or unmoved Super Stoic, and no deity obsessed with his own affronted honor, anxious to destroy all around him. No, his very act of becoming incarnate said he was a God who had tied himself to his creation in a bond he will not break. His was an incarnation that came to its fullness in his going to the cross and from there to immortal glory. His incarnation meant that he was made in the likeness of sinful flesh (Romans 8:3) and so became part of a sinful human family that was under judgement for its sin. Older voices told us that God was impassive, that he couldn't "feel". That he is *so* "other" than we that the obliteration of the human race wouldn't cause the faintest ripple on the surface of his unbroken and transcendent bliss. This is the God and Father of our Lord Jesus Christ? Never! H. R. Mackintosh wanted to know, "When...it is said that God could as easily blot out the world forever as redeem it, we are bound to ask: Could He, if He is like Jesus Christ, who felt He *must* give His life a ransom for many?" Some abstraction that functions as a God might be able to obliterate us but not the God who has actually revealed himself in and as Jesus Christ.

God is certainly other than we. This means he neither has nor can have any love for sin while we (God forgive us) have pampered and nurtured it as though it were a beloved baby. God is infinitely unlike us in our sin but part of that unlikeness is that he will run to redeem us from sin rather than grind us down into it! If we must stress God's "otherness" maybe we should stress that aspect of it for he is so unlike us in our bitterness and in that ungodly way we have of harboring grudges and deliberately isolating fellow-sinners.

The God who revealed himself in Jesus Christ is holy (ethically pure and above us in every conceivable way) and righteous (maintaining his own integrity which is the fountain and shape of all that is good and right). Might we not think that that being the case he would have obliterated us as soon as we dishonored him (because it is what we would do)? That isn't how 1 John 1:9 sees God's response. There he tells us that the holy God who lives in light and hates moral gloom and murkiness is faithful and righteous to forgive the repentant sinners. God *chooses* to be faithful and righteous. He *lives* rather than merely exists. And he eternally chooses to be faithful to himself. A block of ice doesn't choose to be cold but God, in keeping with his dynamic character and nature, chooses to be faithful and righteous. So, the Holy Father who hates moral darkness and in whom there is no darkness at all, how does his insistence on being faithful and righteous show itself? In the gleeful damning of a world that has earned only his condemnation? No, it shows in his faithfully keeping his commitment to his creation. It shows in his freely forgiving the contrite and repentant sinners of all their sins and cleansing them from all their unrighteousness in a holy and righteous forgiveness. This is the God John said was revealed in Jesus Christ (compare 1 John 1:1-2).

The God who reveals himself in Jesus Christ is one who sees his Godhood not as something to be enjoyed in ceaseless self-contemplation or self-congratulation, much less is it to be exploited in some self-centered attitude (Philippians 2:6). Whatever we might think of some theological or philosophical abstraction we give the name "God" to, the true God who showed himself in Christ had a set view about his own deity. Having the mind of Philippians 2:6 in his pre-incarnate form of God, he committed himself to incarnation, humble obedience and death on a cross by the ruling powers.

Robert Browning said that true Godhood looks in sorrow on human need, then feels glad to suffer until gladness blossoms into a rage against the oppressor so that God comes to rescue by suffering with and from and for them.

I think this is the authentic sign and seal
Of Godship, that it ever waxes glad,
And more glad, until gladness blossoms, bursts
Into a rage to suffer for mankind,
And recommence at sorrow: drops like seed
After the blossom, ultimate of all,
Say, does the seed scorn the earth and seek the
   sun?
Surely it has no other end and aim
Then to drop, once more die into the ground,
Taste cold and darkness and oblivion there:
And thence rise, tree-like grow through pain
   to joy,
More joy and most joy--do man good again.

And the Holy Father gives his own public approval of how the Son understands and reveals true Godhood by exalting him and giving him the name "Lord" (Phillipians 2:8-9). As Colin Gunton has reminded us, we learn of the being of God "through the way in which Jesus does the conquering work of the Father." What kind of God is it that conquers rebellious powers by dying on a cross as a young man?

So that when every knee bows and every tongue confesses that Jesus is *Lord* they are embracing the heart of the Father and giving *him* glory. See this in 2:10-11 which quotes Isaiah 45:23. In Isaiah 45:21 God insists that he alone is the Lord and a Savior. In 42:8 God insists, "I am the Lord, that is my

name; my glory I give to no other, nor my praise to idols."
When he exalts Jesus he is doing more than rewarding a
lovely young man; he is approving of the interpretation Jesus
had of true Godhood that led to the incarnation and all that
that implied. He is sharing his glory with another who is really
not "another".

It's critically important for us to understand that the one
exalted as Lord is of the same heart and mind as the heart
and mind that was his self-emptying attitude and led to the
cross. In Jesus, God recognized one who surrendered
reigning power in order to exercise saving and serving power
by the giving of himself. And the wonder of it all is that
reigning power *is* saving and serving power. Nothing has
changed. Lordship *underscores* his eternal character. And the
Holy Father's approval of that character underlines the truth of
what Jesus said in John 14:7-10. "If you've seen me, you've
seen the Father. If you know me, you know the Father." And
since the Holy Spirit shaped his life throughout his earthly
phase and was his minister in his self-offering at the cross
(see Hebrews 9:14)—since that is true we know that the
whole Godhead shares the one heart and mind and character
that is revealed in the crucified Christ. When God comes to us
in the incarnate Christ he is not *slumming.* He is being his
eternal self!

Whatever "self-emptying" (ekenwsen) means in Philippians
2:7 it cannot mean and does not mean that Jesus ceased to
be God. The man Jesus is *always* God being the man Jesus.
He was unceasingly God expressing his Godhood "within the
possibilities of human consciousness and character." (Walter
Moberly, *Atonement and Personality,* page 95.)

In saying he "emptied himself," Paul isn't saying he
emptied himself *of something.* Self-emptying is the description
of what he did in becoming incarnate, humbly obeying and
dying on a Roman cross. Self-emptying is all that, in contrast
to "self-exploitation".

*At no point does he leave behind anything that is essential
to Godhood* for then he would have ceased to be God and

that is *precisely* what we must not claim. That is precisely what Paul would oppose. In Jesus we do not find someone who once *was* God and in some way is no longer God. No, in Jesus Christ, at every point, Paul is insisting, you see *God* interpreting what Godhood means *and interpreting it in terms of a willing and choosing human.* Once more, it is true that Jesus is revealing God but that is only true because in and as Jesus, God is revealing himself and his view of himself.

We built a wall that stretched all the way from Eden to Hell's gates. We shut God and one another out. But one day he came into our world, in and as Jesus of Nazareth, and got his shoulder against the foundation of that wall. And we watched him, his face streaked with spit and sweat and blood, and listened to him groan with the strain as he pushed until the wall came down and the gates of Milton's satanic city of Pandemonium fell off their massive hinges.

And when we asked him, our eyes wide with happy disbelief, why he would go to so much trouble for us he said, "Why, because I am God and you are my beloved children." And when we asked him if all this was not lowering himself he said, "Well, yes and no. No, because believe it or not, this holy, happy longing to do good to the world is who I really am."

The Battle Begins With the Birth of the Dragon Slayer

It's manifestly true that the war to redeem the world had begun long before the Word became flesh but historically the incarnation took place during the reign of the cold and calculating Octavian who later took the name of Augustus. An angel told a young Jewish virgin girl that she would bear a baby that the Holy Spirit would form within her. And from that moment onward the Holy Spirit was ever at his side and ever dwelling within him. The holy, righteous and sinless life of Jesus Christ was shaped by the Holy Spirit who, by his gracious work, worked with the Christ as he offered himself in holiness to the Holy Father throughout his life. And it was this holy life that was poured out as an atoning sacrifice "through the eternal Spirit" (Hebrews 9:14). Hebrews 9:14 is not confined to the moment of his death; it embraces the whole of his life that is _consummated_ in the moment of his death. It was by holy obedience that Jesus neutralized sin (Romans 5:18-19) and it was an obedience "even unto death" (Philippians 2:8).

Acts 10:38 insists that God through the Holy Spirit gave Jesus the power and that he used it for good, in healing and delivering. And Luke 4:16-21 tells that the Holy Spirit anointed Christ and moved him to proclaim good news to the people in trouble and in chains so that without the Holy Spirit the story of Christ would not be as it is. All that to say that the entire Godhead was involved in world redemption.

As by a man sin entered the world so by a man sin would be destroyed (Romans 5:12-19 and compare 1 Corinthians 15:20-22). And as it was by a woman that sin entered the world so it was that by a woman the Savior from sin would enter the world (Galatians 4:4; Genesis 3:15 and compare Revelation 12:1-6 and 1 Timothy 2:15).

As in the movies when the righteous knight rode into the jousts and rang his lance against the shield of the evil one so came humanity's champion. He rang his lance against all the evils and inevitable consequences against which humanity was helpless. Sin, the world, the flesh and the Devil, and suffering and death—all were challenged and challenged in our name. And in our name even the always righteous and good and spiritual law that because of our sin had become a law of sin and death (compare Romans 7:7-8:4)—even that was dealt with and peace was gained for us.

Averting the Wrath of God

"However we are to understand the coming wrath of God, Paul teaches us that it is Christ who delivers us from it."

Averting the Reality in God's Anger

However we are to understand the coming wrath of God Paul teaches us that it is Christ who delivers us from it. In 1 Thessalonians 1:10 (and see 5:9) he reminds these former idolaters that God raised Jesus from the dead "who delivers us from the wrath to come." The crucified and now living Christ daily saves us from our empty and pointless lives by giving us purpose and passion (see 1 Peter 1:18 and Revelation 1:6). But there is a day of judgement ahead for humanity and there will be wrath expressed against those who persist in ungodliness and against those who reject the gospel of Jesus Christ (Romans 2:5 and 2 Thessalonians 1:8-9 illustrate).

We don't like to think of God acting in wrath. But then, again, we don't like anyone acting in wrath if it's against us or those we pity. The whole notion of inflicting pain on someone troubles us unless we are driven to distraction into lashing out at our tormentors. Then we speak of justifiable anger. Because that's how it is with most of us and because we know God doesn't "lash out" at his opponents we're tempted to redefine "wrath" so that it is something other than wrath. It becomes more like self-punishment, it becomes something like *God allowing us to hurt ourselves.* However much truth there is in that kind of talk it fails to accept the plain reading of huge sections of scripture. It fails to take seriously the fact that sin shows itself in our tormenting and oppressing others and not just self-destruction. It's right and it's biblical to urge sinners to flee for refuge in Jesus Christ because of our wickedness. And it's especially the wickedness we perpetrate against the defenseless that deserves punishment (compare Hebrews 6:18 and Revelation 6:12-17).

The Personal Element in God's Anger

The wrath the scriptures warn us about is the wrath *of God* and not some autonomous and mechanical reaction resulting from sinful acts. Pour acid on a piece of material and it eats it away simply as physical cause and effect. A person, to some degree and in some way, disintegrates when he or she sins. That seems clear enough but we're not to suppose that the link between sin and personal or societal disintegration is independent of God. The moral deterioration resulting from sin is a positive and dynamic arrangement initiated and sustained by the will of God. Romans 1:18-32 tells us three times that God "gave them up" to this or that when they spurned him. This was a fatherly and judicial act of God and not something that just "happened".

It is critically important that the wrath of God remain personal rather than mechanical or automatic. As Rabbi Heschel has taught us, a careful reading of Exodus 32:10 stresses the personal involvement of God who decides whether or not, in this case or that, to punish or withhold punishment. Jonah 3:9-10 reveals that God "changed his mind" about punishing Assyria. In Hosea 11:9 he decides not to carry out his fierce anger and in Isaiah 48:9 he delays his wrath for his name's sake. All these texts and more make the point that wrath doesn't operate on a slot-machine model—sin goes in and wrath pours out. Jeremiah 18:1-12 develops this truth for us. Even a surface reading shows us that the Bible is utterly opposed to all views of God that are non-personal. This has ramifications for how we are to understand God's anger but it has consequences for the very heart of the believer's life. Without a personal God prayer is emptied of significance. Prayer becomes nothing more than our expressing our inner tensions, wishes or whatever but there is no communion with anyone. Einstein thought "God" was a name for the harmony and law-abidingness of the universe. Paul Tillich thought "God" was the name we gave to "being" itself (or the basis for "being") but you cannot pray to a harmonious but mindless universe and you can't pray to the great "ground of our being". We might cover over that impossibility by calling these things "God" or even "Father" but that would definitely be Freudian. No, people can have a personal relationship with God and because that's true they can experience the personal anger of God as well as his pleasure.

God's Anger, the Present and the Future

The wrath of God is even now seen in the life of the world in various ways and to varying degrees but there is a coming day of judgement and wrath when all wrongs will be righted and a final decision will be made about our eternal destiny. The cross of Christ (the Christ of the cross) is the means by which God extends grace and life to the human family and if we avoid that ultimate wrath it's because we have been embraced in the redeeming work of Christ.

But there is no claim in scripture that in and since the cross of Christ that God's wrath has been obliterated; that he never expresses wrath toward us. That wouldn't be true because throughout the generations he has expressed his anger (compare Romans 1:18 and simply consult a concordance on the word wrath or anger). Wrath is God's holy response to sin; it is redemptive chastisement to draw us back to him *so that* we will not experience his final and terminal judgement. So when we say that Christ averts the wrath of God we should not mean that God *never* punishes when he sees it to be wise and right.

Why Would God Avert His Anger?

But it's vitally important that we ask why God would bother working to save us from his final and definitive outpouring of wrath. Surely the answer is that if his wrath is not averted we will be eternally the losers. That's true, but why does that matter to him? It's because he doesn't want us to be losers! What moves God to avert his final wrath via Jesus Christ is his generous love and grace toward us. He concludes the entire human race under sin and subject to his wrath that he might have mercy on the entire human race (Romans 11:32). He sent his Son into the world so that the world would not experience his ultimate judgement and anger against the sin of which we have refused to repent (John 3:17 and 12:47).

The Wrath of God is God's Saving Grace at Work

And we need to remember also that God's wrath is not an enemy of his gracious purposes toward us—the reverse is true. The wrath of God is God's stern goodness and love toward the human family. The wrath of God is experienced as unpleasant because it is judgement rather than reward, but it God's grace nevertheless. A loving parent's chastisement of a rebellious child is not vindictiveness nor is it *merely* retribution. It is wise love reaching out in the way that is appropriate under the circumstances.

God's anger, says Heschel, "is a reminder that man is in need of forgiveness, and that forgiveness must not be taken for granted." The God of scripture is a personal God who is affected by how humans treat one another. While he is longsuffering and patient he cannot hold his peace with oppressors and abusers forever. "This is one of the meanings of the anger of God: the end of indifference" (Heschel again). But even when God expresses his anger against, say, Assyria, he means to bring Assyria back into the arena of blessing. And should it be that he must bury the Assyrian empire it is his mercy expressed toward the victims of that oppressive power.

Because the wrath of God is an expression of his redeeming love we should not give the impression that it somehow denies his love and care for us. Given the right circumstances we can depend on God moving against us in anger so that we will not experience his *ultimate* anger.

The Contingent Nature of God's Anger

The wrath of God is *a response* rather than an attribute. People who are morally healthy have the *capacity* to be angry. They don't go around ceaselessly angry though they have the moral capacity to be angry in an appropriate situation. Anger is their response to a deplorable situation but when that situation has been righted the anger is gone even though the capacity for anger remains. So it is with God whose wrath is for a little time while his loving-kindness is everlasting. Psalm 30:5 assures us his "anger is but for a moment, his favor is for a lifetime." And Isaiah 54:7-8 says this, "For a brief moment I abandoned you, but with deep compassion I will bring you back. In a surge of anger I hid my face from you for a moment but with everlasting kindness I will have compassion on you." In 57:16 God says, "I will not accuse forever nor will I always be angry" and be sure to see Isaiah 28:23-29.

Sin troubles God because it not only dishonors him, it makes victims of his beloved human family. When God comes to us in and as Jesus Christ, he sees to it that we need not experience his ultimate wrath which would result in our ultimate loss.

The Rise and Fall of Pandemonium

*"We must understand that this
was not a serendipity nor was
it a minor purpose among many
purposes. Christ came to rescue
and to destroy Satan's kingdom!"*

A Throbbing City Destroyed

In 2 Corinthians 10 Paul said the work of apostles and all those who embrace the truth about Jesus Christ is to bring down forts of folly. It's to wage war, tear down castles of error and undermine cities of falsehood and to bring every falsehood into captivity before the feet of Christ. For evil has its structures and its organization and centers of power.

John Milton's Paradise Lost tells us that Satan and his evil host made war with God, were soundly defeated and cast out of heaven to wander in desolate places. But Satan reorganized and structured an evil "world" of which his newly built city, Pandemonium, was the throbbing center. And every center of power that is opposed to the sovereign Lord and has cast its lot in with the satanic agenda is the enemy of the Christ. And when the Chosen one came he came to deal not only with individuals and their sin but also with vast structures and colossal "cities". He came to tear down Pandemonium and all its satellites.

To think of sin only in terms of the individual is to trivialize the problem we're faced with. It is to make less of the glorious salvation brought to us in Christ. When humans took off on the path of rebellion it affected not only Adam and Eve, it involved all their descendants. Nothing could be the same once our father and mother took that fatal step and the whole world was dragged down with us. Social and religious structures were affected and infected. Like some malignant virus sin corrupted and twisted everything and everyone it touched. Those beings and forces that most affect and exercise power over our lives became vehicles of sin. The effects were cosmic as well as catastrophic.

Whatever the "powers" spoken of in the New Testament are and whatever they were to begin with they became anti-God and needed to be disarmed. They were arrogant so he not only stripped them of their power he made a spectacle of them and brought them to heel (Colossians 2:15). They looked unbeatable and in truth, the human race had found them unbeatable. Crushed and narrowed by them, God's beloved human family (see Acts 17:26-29) was helpless and God stepped in to rescue it.

What were the powers he conquered? Whatever we make of them in Colossians 2:15 we know from 1:16 that God created them and therefore they were not intrinsically evil. They were part of the creation that God looked at and said, "very good." But between the time they came from his heart (Psalm 136:5-9) and his hand and the time Paul wrote, they had been derailed. At some point they began to function as God's enemies and whatever functions as God's enemy must be dealt with and reconciled to him. God's functional enemy is an enemy of itself and everything it was meant to further.

[A perfect illustration of this is the law of God and a specific expression of it—the Jewish torah. The law of God is forever and unchangeably good and spiritual and righteous, enriching life and deepening our relationship with God (Romans 7:12,14,16,25). But "the very commandment that was intended to bring life actually brought death" (7:10). In and of itself the law of God is never anything other than a rich blessing—that's what it exists for, but when sin entered, when we chose to live without God, the law became "a torah of sin and death" (7:11-13,23 and 8:2). The holy law bound us to our sin and the result was curse and death. So did the law itself become evil (7:7,13)? Never, but in a fallen world it functioned as an enemy and it had to be reconciled to God and his redemptive purposes (compare 1 Corinthians 15:56; Galatians 3:10,13; Colossians 1:19-20 and compare Romans 8:1-4). And what is true of the law of God is true of every other expression of God's holy love, generosity and wisdom whether it is governments, economic structures, family structures and even the earth itself. Everything is swept up into our sinful agenda and becomes what it was never meant to be.]

Principalities and powers imply structure and organization and further imply that God didn't create a chaos or a countless number of free-standing units. Like a barely finite number of marbles in a barely limitless bag, all existing but all independent of each other. No, God created an interrelated universe with the full intention that it was to exist in harmony and integration. When things went wrong—when sin entered—the whole creation was affected precisely because it was interrelated.

When sin permeated creation it became a different creation. Not different at the molecular level! The thinking, choosing beings now saw the world as a different place and they now related to it in a different way. A "brave new world" came into existence. As I mentioned earlier, these thinking and choosing beings (visible or invisible) didn't create a physical world; they sinfully restructured God's creation, and that included themselves. What God had created out of holy love, expressing the fullness of his joy and creative power and for the pleasure of his creatures, the creatures re-framed. All his gifts we perverted and began to worship the creation (ourselves included) rather than the creator (Romans 1:18-25). We need to understand this. The "world" that we sinners "created" is actually the world that God created only we see it differently, think of it differently and relate to it differently. It was always intended to be the place where God related to us in holy love and brimming with joy, a place we ruled over honorably and wisely to the glory of God and our own enrichment. In falling into line with the satanic and demonic it became a place of selfishness, self-exaltation, cruelty and exploitation. Our hearts were darkened and our thoughts and behavior expressed that moral and spiritual gloom. We seized self-control, treacherously spurned God and "the world" came into existence. This twisted world, which in part is a "worldview" held by actual people and creates a "worldly" praxis, is dangerous to anyone that sets him or herself against it.

When God looks at the world from this angle he doesn't see it as a mass of free-standing individuals but as one grand army of opposition. It is what the word world (kosmos) suggests, an _ordered_ and _organized_ opposition. Since there is a single and driving force at its corrupt and corrupting center (sin) it has a single "world spirit" that shapes and directs it. It is stronger than the sum total of all the individuals. And the individuals are powerless to stand against it and because this is true there is an inevitability about sin, given the existential reality (compare Matthew 18:7 and 1 Corinthians 11:19). In his *Synonyms* here's how Richard Trench explains two important and related words (world and age):

> Kosmos and *"aion"* (age) are closely related in scripture. Aion is "all that floating mass of thoughts, opinions, maxims, speculations, hopes, impulses, aims, aspirations, at any time current in the world, which may be impossible to seize and accurately define, but which constitute a most real and effective power, being the moral, or immoral, atmosphere which at every moment of our lives we inhale, again inevitably to exhale,—all this is included in the *aion*, which is...the subtle informing spirit of the *kosmos*, or world of men who are living alienated and apart from God."

The principalities and powers are part of that whole anti-God and anti-life structure called "the world" (see 1 John 2:15-16). In the New Testament the world is almost always the world in which humans live and when it is seen as an enemy of God it is the world *of humans* viewed as I've rehearsed above. There are times of course when the world is either the humans or simply the earthly environment in which the humans live. So when we read in a few texts that will follow that Christ overcame the world we are not to think of the planet or the humans as simple realities. We're to think of it as earlier described.

He who said he hadn't come to judge the world (John 3:17; 12:47) spoke of his cross as the hour when the world was judged and the hour that "the prince of this world" was driven out (John 12:20-32 and 16:11). The world with all its perversion and power can frighten us at times, but to a frightened apostolic group Jesus spoke words that put heart in them. He said in the world they were bound to have trouble but they could have peace in him because he had overcome the world (John 16:33). But it is because the world can inflict pain on those who oppose it that such assurance is needed. Worse, it is because the world can pour people into its mold (see J.B. Phillips on Romans 12:2) that we need the assurance that Christ has overcome the world. The world and its prince were powerful enough to get a hold on every individual that entered the human race right from the beginning, until, that is, Jesus came on the scene. In John 14:30, as satanic people come to arrest him and initiate his final ordeal, the Christ says, "the prince of this world is coming. He has no hold on me."

Christ's victory over the world and its prince is spelled out in graphic imagery in the book of Revelation. We hear that he is ruler of the kings of the earth (1:5), that he is King of kings and Lord of lords (17:14 and 19:16). In 12:11, at the conclusion of a tremendous war vision, we learn that Christ's followers overcame the Dragon by the "blood of the Lamb". The means by which God overcame the powers might mystify us but that Christ came to overcome them is no secret at all. We're told that he came to destroy the works of the Devil (1 John 3:8) and we're told that he became one of us so that he might destroy the Devil (Hebrews 2:14). We must understand that this was not a serendipity nor was it a minor purpose among many purposes. Christ came to rescue and to destroy Satan's kingdom!

I don't think we say enough about this. The bulk of what we hear stressed relative to the cross is how Christ came to avert God's wrath; and there can be no argument with that truth. Paul explicitly says that that is why Jesus came, to save us from the wrath to come (1 Thessalonians 1:10 and 5:9). But there is a way of saying that and there is a frequency in saying it that, simply by default, we leave the wrong impression. Christ came in the name of God to bring salvation to the human family and his victory against the powers is for them! The gospel is not solely about God's making sure that his holiness is acknowledged and sin is punished. God's holiness has to be central, but the gospel doesn't leave it there, it relates God's holiness to our rescue. If God were "raw holiness" we could easily imagine that he would obliterate us; but he isn't "raw holiness". The gospel is not that God's holy nature recoils against sin—end of story! It is that God's holy nature recoils against sin *and therefore* he came in Christ (not to condemn us but) to rescue us. He came to take on the world and its powers, to triumph over them *so that* he might save the world.

How the World and the Powers Were Overcome

Colossians 2:15 tells us, "And having disarmed the powers and authorities, he made a public spectacle of them, triumphing over them by the cross." Paul tells us what God did through the Christ and while in some texts he stresses that Christ became Lord of the powers through the resurrection (Ephesians 1:19-22, and see 1 Peter 3:22) in this text the cross is the place of triumph. The world and the powers in the context in which we are speaking are anti-God and anti-life because they are permeated with sin and are the instruments of Sin. Christ triumphs over a sinful reality in the only way that sin can be overcome.

This is not a matter of divine "muscles". Christ doesn't confront the anti-God world and powers with streams of force pouring from his eyes as if he were in some Star Wars movie. He overcame sin in the only way that sin can be overcome—through goodness that is holiness. He lived his life to the glory of his Holy Father and because that was true, always and unceasingly true, the Father made him the "last Adam" and renewed the dominion gift to a new humanity which began with and in the image of Jesus Christ.

From the moment God gave him life in Mary's womb Jesus saw the creation as it was supposed to be. He lived in the world as a child of the Holy Father was supposed to live. To him a tree was what a tree should be, a child was what a child was supposed to be and food and clothing and freedom and pleasure, to him, were all gifts to be enjoyed and shared. He renounced the "worldly" way of seeing the world and he used all the power that God gave him each day to honor his Father and to be a blessing. All this he did because he believed that that is how a child should live before his Holy Father. This is what he felt his Holy Father was due!

The power of the world and its principalities lies in their power to seduce and corrupt. There can be no "sin" in sin that is really _coercion._ The power of evil is not something equivalent to physical force. No one can be _coerced_ into righteousness and no one can be _coerced_ into sin. However carefully we must think this through and express it, we submitted to being "talked into" sinning rather than "made" to sin. There was a point at which we could have said no and didn't. There was a point at which we could have said yes and didn't. (No doubt that point is different depending on our place in life.) When Christ met the world and its powers he defeated it not by creative _force_ but by moral and spiritual power, by holy character. He couldn't simply by force of will dissolve sin in the way he just willed water to become wine, and overcoming Satan had nothing to do with whose mental ligaments were the strongest. (You might be interested in a little thing that I have forthcoming called _Enter the Dragon._ It has something to say about the Devil, his character, limits and how he relates to the world.)

So the Christ defeated and triumphed over the world and the powers with a holy life given in obedience to the Holy Father! Its defeat is holiness outlasting evil, it's moral purity exposing moral corruption and it's holy and generous self-denial fracturing to shreds all sensual greed and self-service. The defeat of the world is truth rising above lies; it's honor, just by its very presence, making treachery shrivel; it's Jesus despising the world's threats, treading on its seductions, majestically dismissing its claims and denouncing its very right to exist. It can only be done when light overcomes gloom, when a holy will asserts itself in God's name against all that dishonors and cheapens and enslaves. However we are to phrase it, that's the nature of its defeat and the world *was* and *is* defeated!

But it took the Christ to do it! It wasn't our books, wasn't our vows, wasn't our churches, wasn't our promises or our moral striving—it wasn't us at all! It *isn't* us at all! He did it! He alone and all by himself and that's why *he* is Lord of all the powers, judge of the world and the one who crushed Satan! A human stood up in the name of God and in the name of a new humanity and fractured the whole damning and damnable satanic kingdom to fragments.

And it was there on the cross that the victory was worked out. Paul looked at the cross, rubbed his eyes, and saw to his happy amazement that there on Christ's cross hung "the world" (Galatians 6:14). Revelation 12:11 reminds us that the disciples overcame Satan "by the blood of the Lamb." Not by his pitying love, not by his warm affection, not by his tolerance and bravery, not by his sweet words and true teaching, but by his blood! All these other things must be taken up into that death or that death has no meaning or atoning value. But all these things must be taken up into his *death* because his death was the crowning moment of his life; it was the point at which he offered all that he was and did and meant to be to his Holy Father. It consummated his life and it brought to focus all he meant to do on our behalf. In and through Jesus Christ it was humanity's finest hour!

Let me quote again Heinrich Heine's description of the feasting gods and the entrance of Christ.

> Then suddenly approached, panting, a pale Jew with drops of blood on his brow, with a crown of thorns on his head, and a great cross laid on his shoulders; and he threw the cross on the high table of the gods so that the golden cups tottered, and the gods became dumb and pale, and grew even paler till at last they melted away into vapor.

No wonder Paul said he would brag on nothing else! It's too bad that we've so often missed the drama in it all. It could be that most of the time preachers are looking to make people teary-eyed when they talk about the cross and I'm sure that that's appropriate at times but we mustn't miss the drama and the clash of worlds that's in it. Whispering about the cross in an auditorium where the lights are turned down and children are hushed may be no bad thing, but this message of the cross has galaxies colliding and empires falling there on that hill. It's just possible that young people lose interest in the "message of the cross" because all the drama and adventure is taken out of it by too steady a diet of preached whimpering and emotional striptease. There's more to the gospel than "moving" people and making them "soar".

The Triumph of the Cross a Cosmic Victory

It's because Christ's cross has cosmic dimensions (note Colossians 1:19-20) that Paul walked through town after town where people were under the dominion of corrupt and corrupting powers beyond their control and pointing to each of them he would say, "Courage! Christ defeated these!" Into Roman garrison towns he'd walk and point at the eagle insignias that proclaimed imperial power and say, "Courage! They've all been defeated in Christ." At least, that's what Paul preached!

We only have to compare what the Priene inscription (dated 9 BC and quoted from at length by Hans-Josef Klauck) had to say about Augustus to get the sense of what the Mediterranean people would have thought when Paul proclaimed Jesus. Paulus Fabius Maximus wanted to create a new calendar that would begin on the 23rd of September, the birthday of Augustus. He said it was difficult to say whether the birthday of the divine emperor had brought more joy or benefit but he was sure that "thanks to him, the whole world presents a different aspect...This is why one may rightly regard that event [Augustus' birthday] as the beginning of life and existence." He goes on to say this:

> Whereas the Providence which has ordered the whole of our life, showing concern and zeal, has ordained the most perfect consummation for human life by giving to it Augustus, by filling him with virtue for doing the work of a benefactor among men, and by sending in him, as it were, a savior for us and those who come after us, to make war to cease, to create order everywhere and whereas the birthday of the God [Augustus] was the beginning for the world of the glad tidings that have come to men through him. Paulus Fabius Maximus, the proconsul of the province has devised a way of honouring Augustus."

Note Maximus' use of "savior" (soter) and "good tidings" (euaggelion) and how he spoke of the emperor as a peace-bringer (Augustus had brought an end to years of civil war and closed the temple of Janus, the god of war). These Greek words are the ones we find used in the New Testament about Jesus Christ. You understand that the claims made on behalf of Julius Caesar and the emperors who arose later where religious and well as political and political as well as religious.

So when in a Roman city (Phillippi) and in a Roman province (Achaia, Corinth) Paul spoke of the death of Christ on a cross everyone knew exactly what he was saying and it must have struck them initially as some kind of madness. This was a death that Rome reserved almost exclusively for those who threatened Rome's right to rule. In 64 BC Crassus crucified 6,000 followers of Spartacus along the main road that led into the city of Rome. And in the year that Christ would have been born (4 BC) Varrus crucified 2,000 Jewish insurrectionists near Magdala in Galiliee, enslaved the inhabitants of Sepphoris and burned it down along with Emmaus. Josephus tells us that the Roman governor, Felix crucified Jewish bandits, "a multitude not to be numbered" and later still Vespasian and then Titus would crucify so many

Jews around rebellious Jerusalem that they would run out of stakes on which to nail them.

In crucifying Christ Rome had given its final word on him and when Paul said that by the cross Jesus became *Lord* and stripped the powers it was a word that put Rome in its place. And it should affect Washington, London and every other civic and political capital of the world. Supreme Court decisions and government bans against the entry of Christ into certain lands or settings only make sense *on the surface*. In light of Paul's proclamation it is laughable and at the same time tragic and catastrophic. Activity like that, ancient or modern, is governments, senators, members of parliament, supreme court and high court judges all throwing their weight behind and becoming instruments of godless agendas. And because the reasons given are to protect the rights of all citizens in light of "the constitution" or "parliamentary democracy" the reasons to thrust Christ out take on a fine polish. But as Daniel 2 and 7 and Revelation 13 and 17 teach us, the power and the agenda of the Dragon made itself visible in the political, social and religious structures that were Rome. Still, Jesus met it all and conquered it all and remains Lord until this very hour. And of all places to reign from—doesn't it make you want to smile a little, at least for a little while—he did it on a hanging tree!

By nailing him to a cross Imperial Rome judged Christ to be an insurrectionist only fit to be slain but he conquered their cross. He did more than that; he used their cross as his ladder to universal Lordship. Commenting on Colossians 2:15 N.T. Wright said,

> These powers, angry at his challenge to their sovereignty, stripped *him* naked, held *him* up to public contempt, and celebrated a triumph over *him*. In one of the most dramatic statements of the paradox of the cross...he (Paul) declares that, on the contrary, on the cross God was stripping *them* naked, was holding *them*

up to public contempt, and leading *them* in his own triumphal procession—in Christ, the crucified Messiah."

The Scandal of the Cross

That was the spellbinding vision that was "publicly exhibited" before our eyes, Paul said to the Galatians (3:1, referring to the Roman policy of leaving corpses to rot there in public). Incredible thought that the conqueror of Rome and all it stood for should be a young Jewish man dying on a cross, streaked with blood, spit and sweat. The Jews looked for a sign. "Give us a sign," they said. "A sign that God is with us and is faithful to his ancient promises." They were sure they knew exactly how that sign would look so when God offered them a Messiah whom they "hanged by the neck until dead" they couldn't believe it and said a message like that was scandalous, an insult! He offered them a Messiah that the Romans humiliated by putting him to death on a cross! "Give us wisdom," the Greeks demanded. "Show us how it can all be justified by reason and commonsense. Answer the questions raised by Socrates and left without satisfactory answers." But who could have reasoned from a young Jewish rabbi, rejected by his own and dying in the dark —who could have reasoned from that to salvation for the world? "Scandalous," said the Jew. "Dumb," said the Greek. "The wisdom and the power of God," said the early church.

For church-going people all this has the right ring of piety but the truth is, if we ever had it we've lost the sense of how scandalous it all is. Imagine Paul walking into the Roman town of Philippi where on every corner in letters thirty feet tall there were signs that said: *Caesar is Lord.* Richard Horsley and his colleagues have reminded us that when a Christian said *Jesus is Lord* she was defying the world and making a political statement as well as a religious one. Paul wasn't setting up religious clubs or theological debating societies and when he said, "Jesus is Lord" he wasn't saying (what he insisted on elsewhere) that Christ was the head of the church. He was doing other than that and he was saying more than that. He was saying the world (so to speak) had changed hands, it was under new management. He was bringing Roman citizenship to a lower level and proclaiming the ultimate importance of heavenly citizenship (Philippians 3:20). To Roman citizens he was saying that the *true* Savior didn't march out of Italy but came from heaven when his people needed saving (3:20). The conniving Jewish leaders who said to Pilate "we have no king but Caesar" had an entirely different message than Paul who went about saying there is another king—Jesus Christ (Acts 17:7).

But why was it that Paul said Jesus was now Lord? Because he emptied himself, became a man and was humbly obedient to God even to the point of bearing Rome's judgement against him on a cross. That? That is where Paul pointed for his proof that Jesus is Lord? But how can that make sense? If he had said it thinking that through the cross Jesus had become the most *inspiring* figure in the world we could make sense of it but that isn't what he preached! He said that on the cross Jesus triumphed over all the principalities and powers and now was the Lord of the world! It isn't hard to see why people would have shaken their heads because we're only convinced of it ourselves when we're in a church building singing hymns. We still worry and vacillate and we have had two thousand years of hearing that Jesus is Lord. At least when a local citizen said "Caesar is Lord!" he had something to point to that made his case clear—raw Roman power.

In his biography of his father-in-law, *Julius Agricola,* the Roman historian Tacitus "reports" the speech of Calgacus the British Caledonian warlord to his fellow Britons. "The Romans are the plunderers of the world...If the enemy is rich, they are rapacious, if poor they lust for dominion. Not East, not West has sated them...They rob, butcher, plunder, and call it 'empire'; and where they make a desolation they call it 'peace'." Bitter enough and true enough; but at least it was something you could point to, something you could see and say, "Look, that proves that Caesar is Lord." Brutal and war-hardened Roman legionnaires on the march, towns in flames, raped women, plundered cities, endless lines of slaves and genocide are solid proof about who has the power. And here is Paul, striding into a Roman province like Achaia or into a Roman city like Phillippi or even into Rome itself with what?

The story of a public lynching on a public gallows!

A case in which a lynch-mob had its own brainless and heartless way one Friday over at a spot called Skull Hill.

A young Jewish man was rushed to the hanging tree and left swinging in the breeze while the gutless Roman judge gave his wife a shifty-eyed look and the Jewish mob-leaders glanced at each other in grim satisfaction as…ahem…as they headed back to worship the one true God in spirit and in truth.

Am I forgetting the resurrection? No, we mustn't do that but we must allow the exaltation of Jesus to his place as Lord to rise out of the soil Paul placed it in. The incarnation and humble obedience to the point of dying on the cross are what Paul means by "self-emptying" in Philippians 2:5-8 and it is *because of these* ("therefore") Jesus Christ is (resurrected and) exalted to Lordship (2:9-11). In the redemptive drama it wasn't at the resurrection that Christ said no to the world and the evil powers. It was at the cross and that's why God raised him because death had no right to hold him (Acts 2:24).

Give us a sign, they said, that Jesus is Lord. They were looking for "successful power". Give us a sign, we say, that Jesus is Lord and smile when verses about the cross are quoted. But when ungodly principalities and powers persecute our lovely brothers and sisters the first thing we do is appeal to Caesar. "Lay sanctions on them," or "send in the troops" or "make a desolation and call it peace." Are these the weapons by which Paul brought down forts and strongholds that set themselves against God? In 2 Corinthians 10:3-5 he said he had other weapons. "Give us power," we plead and think of the might of economics, armies, nuclear weapons and brilliant scientists. *But power to do what?* What sword or smart-bomb or economic shrewdness can make people captives of Jesus

Christ? What legions can conquer a man or a woman's sin and bring them in humility and devotion to the feet of Christ? Is that the power we seek?

The Continuing Scandal of the Cross

But if Christ has triumphed over the world and its powers how is it that they are still very much alive and well? What has changed in 2,000 years of Christianity? One of the things that plagued the Scottish commentator Marcus Dods was "the ineffectiveness of Christianity." Matthew Arnold, the poet and literary critic, who in matters of faith lost his way, wrote that sad poem *Dover Beach* about the failure of happy dreams and of the failure of the Christian faith despite a promising beginning.

> The sea of faith
> Was once, too, at the full, and round earth's shore
> Lay like the folds of a bright girdle furl'd;
> But now I only hear
> Its melancholy, long, withdrawing roar,
> Retreating to the breath
> Of the night-wind down the vast edges drear
> And naked shingles of the world.

And how many today, do you suppose, haven't at some point looked long and hard at the world and wondered what difference the gospel has made? And when we read the small print of many a sermon or press a preacher hard, examining his claim that Jesus is Lord, we note the hemming and hawing. Never mind looking around the world as a whole, what about looking at our own families and even closer home, what about looking within our hearts. In there, where after years of Bible reading, fervent prayers, passionate hymn-singing and conferences by the train-load we still find peevishness and meanness close to the surface. And what of churches that are fed the best kind of food and challenged with the most glorious challenges but remain the same petty and selfish little gatherings? So whether we survey the planet or inspect a single heart the message seems plain—not much change here! What does all this say to us?

Whatever else it says it makes this crystal clear: we didn't overcome the world!

God gave us dominion over the creation and over ourselves (Genesis 1:26-28 and Psalm 8:1-9) and we became treacherous and perverse—generation after generation until we became so patterned in sin that we are called "sinful flesh" –the sinning people (Romans 8:3). But one day one of us (yes!) stood up and said no to sin and yes to holiness, said it in every conceivable way and used such power as God gave him to glorify God and bless the world around him. He, and he alone, confronted the world and stopped it dead in its tracks and God finally had one who knew what to do with power and dominion so he gave him all power! And now a new Adam, the head and beginning of a new humanity is Lord of all.

Yes, yes, but what difference does it make? The vast mass of corruption still breeds and thrives at a cosmic level and we at the individual level have our interminable brawls with skewed relationships. All this is proof that we haven't triumphed over the powers but is it proof that Christ didn't triumph over them? That's the fundamental question. It isn't that we by moral excellence and attainment defeated the powers but did he? The fact that we ceaselessly brawl with the powers rather than tamely and with a whimper submit to them is proof of something else. It proves that no matter how often they cut and beat us till we cry out in our shame we stubbornly believe that Christ is Lord of them and that he's against them. And if he's against them then so are we! And our losses remind us how deep the smog that is sin has penetrated into our racial lungs so that we breathe it without effort and hardly know what it is to draw a clean breath. So when we look at Jesus we're filled with awe at his purity and righteousness and when we call him a "great" Savior we know exactly what we mean.

Yes, yes, but what difference does it make?

The cross of Jesus Christ stands an eternal judgement on evil and it assures us that at the heart of the universe is a holy Lord that has conquered Sin. We're given assurance that righteousness triumphs over evil. And it assures us that that triumph is not guaranteed because we are against it but because he is against it! The cross proclaims to us that all wrongs will be righted!

But if he has defeated the world and the evil powers why do they still exist? They still exist because the defeat of "the world" is not its obliteration. As long as there are sinners "the world" will exist. Every generation of sinners constructs this anti-God empire and that kind of constructing will only end when God brings an end to the sinful people that build it. So the world has not been defeated? It has been defeated! If Jesus were born today he would meet the same "world" he met back in the first century—there's no new world, and the judgement with which he judged it back then is an eternal one! But more than that, an individual conquered it. The victory over the world is Jesus' victory. As an individual he met and conquered sin, suffering, and death! For him, as an individual, death is no more and his connection with sin has been eternally severed (note 2 Timothy 1:10 and Romans 6:9-10 and Hebrews 9:25-28).

And the great news about the good news is this—he did it in our name! Sin has been eternally dealt with in that individual called Jesus Christ! His personal and individual experience (a present reality for him), he will one day make *our* personal and individual experience. The existence of evil does not mean he hasn't conquered it. The existence of the world does not mean he hasn't conquered it. The existence of sin, suffering and death does not mean he hasn't conquered them. The existence of his enemies does not mean he hasn't conquered them. Now the Lord of all, he uses all of them to gain his purposes while he brings the whole cosmos to a grand and glorious finale. If the existence of evil in the world proved that Christ was not Lord it would prove that God had never been in control of the world because evil has been with us from the Garden. There were those who wondered why everything continued as it was from ancient times and no final righting of wrongs had taken place (see 2 Peter 3:1-3 and how Peter responds with 3:8-9). God isn't slack about promises but is longsuffering and wants people to come to him for salvation. The existence of enemies doesn't prove Christ isn't Lord, because he "reigns in the midst of his enemies" (Psalm 110:2, a psalm quoted repeatedly concerning Christ in the New Testament).

Where then is our comfort, the inspiration to take the battle to the enemy? It's in this that Jesus Christ has personally met and conquered all that stands opposed to God and his eternal purposes for his creation. And he did it in our name and for our sake. That Jesus is Lord is not just a religious claim, it is political to the core. The enemies he overcame were not simply invisible powers but the visible realities in which those invisible powers acted in the world.

So, has sinned been neutralized? Yes. Has the world and the powers been exposed and defeated? Yes. Have suffering and death been abolished and immortality arrived? Yes. Where then? In the personal and individual experience of Jesus Christ. For him there is no more sin, suffering, or death. In and for him a new world has actually begun and there is literally no more death (2 Timothy 1:9-10). And this human is the first of a new humanity and when he has completed his present reign in the midst of his enemies he will make his own individual experience the experience of the new humanity he has created and shaped. Everyone embraced in his redeeming work will be part of a new humanity and they will reign with him (Romans 8:17) over a redeemed creation (8:18-23). All this is accomplished fact for Jesus Christ and for those who are his it exists by faith (compare Hebrews 11:1).

Scholars speak of eschatology in terms of an "already" and "not yet". This is surely true. But the already is definitely already in the experience of Christ and the "not yet" relates to our individual and complete experience of what he already experiences. The world and all the powers have been overcome—that is a past event because Jesus is now Lord!

And if you think the scandal of the cross exists only for those who are enemies of Jesus Christ you're out of touch with reality. Believers suffer as much and as severely as non-believers (depending on where they live in the world) and in their pain they too ask for a sign. "Make sense of our suffering," they plead and God offers them the cross of Christ. But that makes no sense! We want our suffering to be taken seriously, we want our suffering and loss to be explained to our satisfaction and God offers us the cross of Christ. But that makes no sense!

It might make no sense because we don't understand the cross. Maybe if we took a headlong dive into the meaning of the cross and didn't come up for air until we were loaded with treasure...Maybe we'll break the surface with eyes shining with excitement and broken hearts mysteriously healed. But in my own experience, one tiny little life's experience, do you know who finds all that most offensive? Ministers of the Word.

Greater is he that is in you

John in first John speaks of believers as overcomers. He speaks of them overcoming the "evil one" and "the world" (see 2:13-14; 4:4; 5:3-5). He uses various tenses to stress the nature of the overcoming. He uses aorists in the indicative to express a deed completed. He uses the perfect to stress that the deed accomplished in the past still stands as done! He uses presents tenses and participles to say that the overcoming in an ongoing experience and (probably) uses the present participle as an adjective to describe the overcomer (as a believer in the incarnate Christ).

It is true that only Jesus Christ has personally and individually overcome the world and the evil one, and John knows that very well. But John insists that *in Christ* we overcome the world also. He insists that *in Christ* who is our representative we overcame the world at the cross and that when by faith we entered into union with that overcoming

Christ we too became victors. We too continue to experience the victory over the world that Jesus alone has accomplished because by becoming one with him by faith we are part of him.

Of course there's a day coming when all vestiges and appearance of the world and the evil one will be obliterated but the victory isn't postponed until then! The present victory is only fully expressed then. Even *now* faith is the victory that overcomes the world because the object of our faith is a person and that person has overcome the world and made a spectacle of it! *This is the gospel!*

If I were a younger fellow and I'm not and if I were into wearing tee-shirts and I'm not and if I were into having stuff printed on tee-shirts and I'm not—but if I were, I'd probably have this printed on one: aute estin h nikh h nikhsasa ton kosmon h pistis hmwn!

And it doesn't matter that it doesn't look like that in our day by day plodding through life. It doesn't matter that our emotions deny that we've overcome the world or if moral defeats dog our every step and evil seems to have the upper hand in life. There are only two questions that matter. Did Jesus Christ overcome the world and do we believe in him? Future days will show beyond possibility of doubt that faith *is* the reality of the things we hope for. *This is the victory that overcomes the world, our faith in the victorious Lord Jesus Christ.*

Unmasking A Predatory Alien

"To look to Man for the cure
is profoundly wrong-headed
because it is Man without God
that is the problem"

The Enlightened West and the Dismissal of "Sin"

John Lennon's haunting song 'Imagine' is a musical version of a much older claim that all we need is Man. We don't need God, religion or any such crutch; if only Man would behave we'd have paradise here on earth and an endless sleep at the end of life. In the 1800's, Man's love affair with himself was in full flow and the scientists and philosophers assured us that progress was inevitable because every day and in every way we were getting better and better. No one can read (and now enjoy the benefits) of the tremendous strides made in those Enlightenment years without being pleased and grateful. The marvelous progress and benefits weren't the problem. Man had fallen again to the temptation of pride and the self-sufficiency that is its twin. We were sure our inventions, our greater learning, our understanding of the heavens, our unmasking and conquering of bacteria and our moral advances had nothing to do with God. They were our work! In fact, some of it could only have taken place when we were brave enough and willing to kick God out and take responsibility for ourselves. The "new birth" we had needed was the Renaissance and the benefits really showed themselves in the Enlightenment. Given time, Man would entirely remove the curse from the world and earth would become heaven. Genesis 3—11 was back with a vengeance.

In the story I read years ago, the little German girl had been raised in a careful home that took God seriously—so when she visited her grand-uncle's home she expected they would give thanks before eating. When the old man told everyone to start eating without saying grace she wanted to know why they hadn't thanked God. Without a second's hesitation the hard-working farmer told her, "Ich bin Gott!" And there lies the end of temptation, there lies the result of blessedness without the recognition of dependence or thankfulness—I am God!

The Lennon song in its day, to many of us who were taken by its wistful appeal, sounded just right with its non-violent vision of utopia. But it was a moving presentation of a humanistic dream that had been exposed as shallow religion (yes!) and a Pollyanna-ish refusal to face reality. It repeated the sentimental and naive murmur of the pre-World War I poem that went:

> So many gods, so many creeds,
>   So many paths that wind and wind,
> While just the art of being kind
>   Is all the sad world needs.

Well, of course, but isn't that precisely the problem? The cosmic disease that believers call sin can't be diagnosed in this shallow fashion; it's too deeply rooted and radical for that. Contrast that diagnosis with Paul's in Romans 7:14-23. As J.S. Whale remarked, the poem's like saying all a man in a Nazi labor camp needs is the train fare home. You might remember the story of the desperate man who went to his therapist for help because his life was a shambles. His advisor told him to go home and pull himself together and the patient told him, "That's why I'm here. The thing I pull myself together with is busted." The sweet little poem lost its charm with the use of the newly invented airplane to bomb fleeing children in Spain, mustard gas, and World War I. Twenty million dead and hundreds of millions inconsolable! John Lennon's hope in man without God had already shown itself in the horror of the Nazi labor and extermination camps, gifted surgeons doing the unspeakable in the name of medical advance and patriotism and surrounding townspeople and villagers pretending they didn't know what was going on. The allied treatment of Germany at Versailles and in the years that followed, made World War II virtually inevitable and man's kindness was again conspicuous by its absence. These wars, with the butchering of countless Chinese civilians by invading Japanese armies, Britain's fire-bombing of civilian Dresden and Hamburg and America's nuclear bombing of Hiroshima and in the wake of it all the horrible gulags, further genocide, the manufacturing of famines and the starving of millions expose our sinfulness. We don't only do these things to our enemies we do them to our neighbors and even to our own families and friends. We didn't do them only in the "primitive" years we do them now in the era of moral, medical, scientific and social sophistication. In all this the foundations of the doctrine of "inevitable progress" and the boundless optimism that rest on Man are one more time laid bare and seen to be rotten.

The problem doesn't lie in John Lennon's desire for non-violence, brotherhood and his call that we should refuse to settle for the human tragedy that exists—that's not to be criticized. But the search for the cure is conducted in the wrong place and out of the wrong convictions. To look to Man for the cure is profoundly wrong-headed because it is Man without God that is the problem. Man is the problem not only because he is the sinner but also because part of his sin is that he cannot and will not see that he is central to the problem and cannot redeem himself.

You understand I'm not suggesting that we should accept the bleak picture and say that Man is no part of the cure. I'm saying that as long as we underestimate our desperate situation and look to ourselves as gods we perpetuate the problem. Our central crime against God (and therefore against ourselves) is rejecting him in our blind arrogance and claiming we are the cure rather than the disease. We insist on searching among the dead for someone to bring us life when we've been told repeatedly that the only one who can bring us life is not in the tomb because "he has risen." Someone recently sent me a piece of Dakota Indian wisdom that said when you find yourself riding a dead horse you should recognize that that's the case and get another horse. He went on to say that the big, modern and wise Western world ignores this. Instead we flog the dead horse harder or buy a new whip or try a new rider or redefine "dead". Or we harness several dead horses together to see if they'll go faster or do studies about how other countries ride horses or we lower the expectations so that the dead horse can be included in whatever structure we come up with. Depending on ourselves without God for a better world is to sit astride a dead horse and whip him harder.

But there's another thing to be considered here. The promise of a possible utopia without God has nothing for the countless millions of past generations that were victims of "bad luck" and inhuman treatment. There's no utopia for them! One of these days, maybe, in some far off future, perhaps, before earth's resources are depleted beyond recovery, a relative handful will enjoy a peace and prosperity that they have created for themselves. And what of the countless victims that were sinned against and the vast number of powerful predators who made their lives a living hell, predators who found their pleasure in the agony of the victims? Imagine is easier to sing if you're wealthy and healthy and your family is well catered for and if you're singing to those who can afford to buy your recordings. But without God we can sing no wistful and half-hopeful songs for the countless millions that suffered and died in misery under savage oppression. It's too late for them! How can we take pleasure in a philosophy that dooms billions to eternal injustice?

Sin Dismissed In Pursuit of Pleasure

But I suppose that the most common face of the sin problem that we see in the West (though it's fed by philosophy and cultural convictions) is the selfish pursuit of pleasure and comfort. There is little thought of God or sin or holiness until old age and death come close. We do what pleases us and as for God and the rest of the world, well, they will have to struggle on as best they can. Most of us, I suppose, wouldn't dream of thinking we were gods but we definitely claim and exercise the right to dismiss the one true God and in this we make ourselves an end in ourselves. We're back at Genesis 3—11 where, well-fed, housed and healthy, we curl up in front of a nice fire with a mirror so we can go on adoring ourselves.

Irish singer Bob Geldof took financial aid to needy peoples of the world at the time Michael Jackson inspired vast contributions to the starving third world with his song We Are the World. Geldof made further visits and sincerely lamented the torment of nations ravaged by years of wars, famines and stolen aid. To dismiss his work on behalf of these poor people would be unchristian and bitter rubbish indeed. But on a talk show Geldof claimed there is no life after death, that the grave is the end of us and said that he was pleased it was so. Here's this rich, healthy and well-received man who wants nothing to do with God and will be quite happy to begin an eternal sleep. But what of the masses he had seen (and the countless dead before them) and what of the war-lords who ate their flesh and drank their blood? Geldof is pleased that there is no God or life after death. This too is sin! For anyone who is pleased that there is no justice, no righting of wrongs and no hope for tormented millions is selfish to the core! Let me repeat, God has done compassionate things through Geldof and people like him, things that are not to be sneered at. Tight-fisted believers who cluck their tongues at unbelief have Christ and Matthew 25:31-46 staring them in the face. I don't suppose those of us who can't be troubled to give a helping hand will want to meet Geldof in the line approaching the judgement seat. But then Bob, sadly, will have troubles of his own.

Various Responses to Sin Among Believers

There is a way to appreciate salvation that casts a bright light on the nature of sin and some down the years have had much to teach us simply by the way they confessed their sin. John Wesley urged John Haime to keep a journal and he did and in it he wrote, "I was hastening on to eternal destruction when the great tremendous God met me as a lion in the way." Isn't there something majestic about that? Something majestic about a God who comes to meet us on the road to destruction that we're hurrying down? And what does it reveal about the nature of sin?

And here's what Sampson Staniforth said. "I went to my tent that night, seeing all my sins stand in battle array against me." How different those confessions are to those we hear so often today.

The Holy Blabber and the One Sentence Cover-All

Sometimes, with so many gory details matter-of-factly thrown in it can sound like a "True Confessions" magazine or "holy blabbing" rather than a penitent sinner confessing sin against the Holy Father. On the other end of the spectrum there is the "generalized" sentence-long and cover-all admission that we "have sinned". The "holy blabbing" type at best tends to rivet the attention on the social specifics of the sin rather than the awful *character* of sin and the cover-all is a confession anyone can, most everyone does and everyone should make. Trust me at this point, I think I really *do* understand that how we word the confession is not the be-all or end-all of the matter. But it is so often the case that our speech is shaped by our inner sense of things and the prevailing culture that we need to reflect carefully on this matter of public or private confession.

The Prisoners of Conscience

Then there are the sinners who are so guilt-ridden that they cannot cease from reflecting on the great wrong of their wrong. In a most unhealthy sense David's healthy words becomes theirs: "My sin is ever before me." In part they do this because their inner world is so shaped that they do it without thinking about it; it is no *choice* because it has become a compulsion. And that inner shaping is the result (in part) of what they've been long taught: if you are truly repentant you will continually agonize over your sin. Their conscience is like a bell buoy that mournfully clangs with the least emotional ripple. They *can't* just walk away from it after an honest and appropriate confession because to do that, they've been assured, would mean they weren't very sorry for what they've done. Harry E. Fosdick thought the conscience was like a car horn—its business was to sound a warning. When a car horn is jammed it is one unending blare that is no longer useful, but at least everyone knows it's malfunctioning. When a conscience jams, the poor tormented soul thinks it's the voice of God and lives in misery as well as in slavish fear of God. The ceaseless strident wail drowns out even the voice of God that is offering forgiveness.

The Unforgivable Nature of Sin

How vulnerable we are, we sinners. In the hands of lord Sin even the noble thing within us is bent to his destructive agenda. Tell people the truth that sin is the one unendurable before God and a host of convicted sinners worry themselves sick wondering (and often denying) that sin can be forgiven. In strict logic this paradox may be difficult to work out (some say impossible) but in daily life we get clues as to how love and sin can be worked out. Certainly in the person of God we hear the two truths affirmed: sin is inexpressibly evil and the holy God so loves that he forgives it. I don't know of any more revealing discussion of the destructiveness of unforgiven sin than Hawthorne's book The Scarlet Letter. This only adds misery to the misery of those whose conscience is jammed because it has gone beyond hypersensitivity and now approaches despair.

We need to insist that Jesus died to enable us to live for righteousness (1 Peter 2:24) and no longer unto ourselves but unto him that died and rose again (2 Corinthians 5:15). But it is vitally important for us to understand and believe that Christ "gave himself for our sins" that he might deliver us (Galatians 1:4). And it's essential that we take God's word for it, that in Christ we have "the forgiveness of our trespasses" (Ephesians 1:7) in keeping with the richness of his grace. And as Luther reminded us, "Christ was given, not for feigned or counterfeit sins, nor yet for small sins, but for great and huge sins; not for one or two, but for all; not for vanquished sins...but for invincible sins." I've no wish to be rude here, only to be plain, but there comes a point when it isn't humility that claims our sins are too great to be forgiven. At some point it becomes an offense to God who continues to give us his word that in Christ all our sin is freely and fully forgiven. In refusing to rest in his forgiveness, we only add that sin to other sin. If God's love in the cross of Christ doesn't persuade us that our sin is forgiven it is no longer ourselves we our despising, it is the cross. (I beg you, seek forgiveness from God who is not only able but eager to forgive!)

The Devil Made Me Do It

Johann Goethe in his masterpiece, the extended poem Faust, paints a rivetingly clear picture of how we place the blame on others for our sins. Faust makes a bargain with the Devil (Mephistopheles) and enters into the depths of sin. At no time does Mephistopheles coerce the philosopher, it's always persuasion and seduction, and it is always with Faust's agreement. The doctor doesn't sink like a lump of lead, however, for he has moments when his conscience rises up like a flood and in anger he curses the Devil for bringing him into such a state. But the jeering Devil reminds him more than once that it was Faust that called him and not he that called Faust. And when Faust, who had seduced an innocent girl, curses Mephistopheles as a "snake of snakes" and "damnable villain" the Devil scornfully reminds him that he has "quite a gift for devilment." Faust wasn't made to sin and once having entered the business he showed that he was eager to get on with it. And it's no accident that in the Bible Satan, is repeatedly associated with the crafty serpent whose name is Deceiver and not Coercer.

In this world of ours sin is inevitable (though it is no necessity) but it isn't Satan that makes it inevitable. The scriptures link Satan with human sin and of that there's no doubt. But our hearts are deceptive (said Jeremiah) and we're always ready to blame someone or something else for our sin. Adam blamed the woman God gave him and the woman blamed the serpent, and on it goes. There are those who think that if we don't take Satan seriously we aren't taking sin seriously. There may be some truth in that but this going on and on about Satan and his countless hordes of demonic servants may be one more way to shrug off the responsibility for our sins. (And the breezy way that some make public confession doesn't seem at all healthy.) I'm one of those that think if the Devil and all the satanic hordes dropped down stone-dead this moment that sin would continue. Satan too was overcome by Sin and is a fellow-sinner with us. Sin is his lord rather than his being the author and creator of sin.

Righteousness cannot truly be "righteousness" if we are overwhelmingly compelled to behave righteously or to be righteous and sin isn't "sin" if we're made to sin. Filling every square foot of space with demons that can get into our minds and deposits sinful thoughts there as a cuckoo lays its eggs in another's nest may be nothing more than more ducking and diving out from under our responsibility. (God enabling I'll have a little book that offers some proposals about Satan. It'll be called He that is in the World. You might find that useful.)

Sin as a Pervasive Power

In Romans 5—7 Paul characterizes sin as a slave-owner, a king reigning over a kingdom and a lawgiver. He personifies sin (gives it a capital S, so to speak) which enables him to tell us truths about it more vividly and more easily. Sin is presented as more than wrongs committed by individuals or the human family as a whole; it is presented as a power that pervades the whole human scene. We might speak of it as a "thinking virus" that plots its agenda and moves from host to host, infecting as it goes until the whole human race is diseased. Or a fungus that pollutes as it spreads, making everything unclean and loathsome. Or maybe a thick blanket of poisonous smog shrouding our spinning planet. We're born into such a world and as soon as we're born we begin to breathe the poison. And before long we're coughing into the air our own configured moral germs from diseased lungs, polluting the environment further and making sure that the yet unborn will join us in our sin-sickness. No wonder David, in moral agony of repentance, linked his abominable crimes against God, Uriah and Bathsheba with the very beginning of his life (Psalm 51:5).

When the sinless, holy and righteous Christ offered himself as an atoning sacrifice to deal with sin, it wasn't just individual sins he was dealing with and it wasn't only individual temptations he was conquering; he was overcoming the smog, he was destroying the kingdom of Sin! He came into our world as one of us and resisted the infection because with the aid of the Spirit of God he ceaselessly chose to be healthy. (The English words holiness and health come from the same root.) Sin could not make him sick. Nor would he accept its kingship or submit to its law or put his neck under its yoke. He defied the power and delivers others from it! And beyond forgiveness he is working and will complete in our experience a total moral transformation and the utter destruction of sin.

Sin is a Human Affair

The cross wasn't the act of a handful of us—we all had a hand in it. It wasn't just those who were present on that day giving their voice to the young man's execution. If the human family had not corrupted itself for millennia this would never have come to pass. Peter and Paul saw the cross of Christ as the inevitable result of the sinful apostasy that corrupted us all. I forget who said it but he was right. *"Sin didn't begin with me and it will not end with me."*

This means that the atoning/reconciling process is to be seen as a single movement and accomplishment—it deals with sins because it deals with Sin; it deals with an individual's sins because it deals with the sins of the whole family. The cross is not only an event at a particular time in history; it is a timeless deed that in principle deals with the sin of the human family, past, present and future. It dealt with sins that were not even yet committed as well as those committed in ages past (note Hebrews 9:15). It's true that God sees us sinning as individuals but he sees us sinning *as individual members of a single family.* The 1st century cross deals with the sin of every century because the sinners of every century constitute a single family. The scope of redemption is racial because our sin is racial.

Our Sinful Inter-Relatedness

In personal experience we haven't all sinned in the same way and to the same degree in specifics but we have all of us fallen in sin one way or another. And in our sinning we have made it easier for others to sin as others have made it easier for us to sin. Sin is like a contagion and spreads like a virus. It pollutes and spreads pollution as it goes. When Paul in Romans 3:9-18 gives the verdict on the Jewish nation and says "there is none righteous, no not one" he is speaking the broad truth. He made the point the Bible never tires of making; the human family is in the sinning business as a family.

We tend to see sin as an endless series of individual wrongs by individual people. There's truth in that, of course, but it's not the whole picture. Biblically, any sin and all sins are linked together and related to the original human rebellion (Genesis 3—11) against God that triggered God's loving wrath. In scripture, while individual sins are certainly taken into account, sins are seen as part of a universal network—they are seen as part of a single rebellion by a single human family. We see this in the way the prophets link human sin in various eras with the original human rebellion and its consequences. In doing this they remind us that we're a single human family that sins as a human *family.*

Take Jeremiah 4 for example. The entire chapter makes it clear that Jerusalem and Judah are being addressed (see 4:3-5,11,16 and elsewhere) but when judgement is described it is outlined in terms of Genesis 3-11. In 4:23-25 the judgement against Judah is a return to pre-creation conditions. You'll remember how the beginning chapter of Genesis shows God at work shaping, blessing and filling the place with life and harmony. In response to our rebellion the world was to take on wilderness characteristics (Genesis 3:17-19; 4:29 with Jeremiah 4:26). God becomes a destroyer instead of a life-giver, a bringer of chaos instead of harmony. But this is in response to human rebellion. The Jeremiah 4 text links the sin of Judah in the 7th century with the original rebellion of Genesis 3—11.

The Christ himself does that very thing in Matthew 23:29-36. There he identifies his own generation with previous generations of the rebellious. His sinful peers are true sons of their sinful fathers (23:31) and Christ attributes to his peers the killing of Zechariah (23:35, "you" murdered). But he does more than that; he goes all the way back to our original rebellion and claims that all the righteous blood shed on the earth from Abel until Zechariah (whose death is in 2 Chronicles, the last book in the Hebrew Bible) would come on that generation.

Why would he say such a thing? His peers hadn't been born then so how could he hold them responsible for crimes they didn't commit? Christ was doing what prophets before him often did; he was linking the present sinful rebellion with the original sinful rebellion and making it one grand narrative of evil. In his murderous peers Cain is alive again. In his murderous peers the murderous fathers still lived. (It isn't a matter of transferring guilt—guilt can't be transferred—it's a matter of sinful identification with the human rebellion that is truly only one grand criminal revolt.) See this in texts like Zephaniah 1:2-4; Isaiah 13:9-13; Exodus 1—14 and elsewhere.

Recognizing the community nature of sin is important to us. In addition to opening our eyes to better understand the atonement, it's an antidote against self-righteousness. Upright individuals tend to think of themselves a cut above other sinners. They tend not to think of the moral advantages they have had and the moral disadvantages experienced by those who have been raised in moral filth and squalor. In this way the upright tend to rate themselves too highly and self-righteousness is nurtured. See Titus 3:2-3. To understand, for good or ill that we are a single family, is a great leveler.

Sin is Personal Pollution As Well As Relational Infidelity

It's perfectly legitimate (because it's biblical) to speak of sin as breaking the law of the Holy Father but we need to remember that the scriptures speak of sin as pollution and uncleanness also. In the Old Testament disease and some physical conditions required atonement by a sin offering. When such sacrifices were offered we're told that the sin was forgiven and that the sinner was cleansed or purified. When we break the Holy Father's law we incur more than guilt. That relational infidelity does something to our character as well as to our status before him. The scriptures speak of things like hardening, pollution and bent-ness. We not only sin, we become sinners and sinful, terms that speak of our condition and attitude in addition to our status as guilty. In the beginning we became sinners because we sinned but as we continued in sin then we sinned because we were sinners. Specific acts of sin arise out of our twisted and contaminated inner structure as Christ has taught us in Matthew 15 when he says that all evils arise out of the heart. (The truth that sin is soul pollution as well as guilt should make us slow to say that our sin was transferred to Christ.)

Sin and Its Cosmic Effects

We normally think of the effects sin has within us as individual humans and human communities, which certainly makes sense; its polluting effect on us can hardly be overstated. But sins affects more than the human element in creation because Colossians 1:19-20 says that "all things in heaven and on earth" needed to be reconciled to God. Here's what it says: "For God was pleased...through him to reconcile to himself all things, whether things on earth or things in heaven, by making peace through his blood, shed on the cross." (Compare Ephesians 1:9-10 on this.)

Whatever we make of the Colossians text it shows plainly enough that with the entrance and presence of sin the whole creation was thrown into some kind of alienation from God. Something like that is involved in what Mesillat Yesharim said (as quoted by Cornelius Plantinga). "If a man is allured by the things of this world and is estranged from his Creator, it is not he alone who is corrupted, but the whole world is corrupted with him." The sinful human condition is a sign of a wider derangement and chaos. Dachau and Auschwitz say something about distant galaxies and Jupiter probes and Papa Doc's Haiti says something about a whole creation that groans and longs for redemption (compare Romans 8:18-21 and Ephesians 3:10). The creation and we are under bondage together.

Pragmatist and psychologist William James who wouldn't at all have shared the central proposals expressed in this book, was shaped more than he knew or cared to admit by the Christian faith. He thought life was worth living, from the moral point of view, since it is what we make it. So he thought our moral struggle had profound worth. He goes on to say this:

> For my own part, I do not know what the sweat and blood and tragedy of this life mean, if they mean anything short of this. If this life be not a real fight, in which something is eternally gained for the universe by success, it is no better

that a game of private theatricals from which one may withdraw at will. But it *feels* like a real fight, as if there were something really wild in the universe which we...are needed to redeem.

All things have been restored and "re-created" in Christ who is the representative of the new and true humanity (the last Adam, the image of God—Colossians 1:15, Genesis 1:26 and 1 Corinthians 15:45). Whatever else we should say about all this, this much is true: our sin in some way unhinged the creation or it wouldn't have needed to be restored or reconciled to God. Sin affected the farthest star. We're reminded of this when nations like Babylon, Edom or Judah sinned and God's response is "uncreation". In literal fact "uncreation" didn't take place with the judgement on these nations but the description of undone heavens, an unformed earth, birdless skies and fishless seas points us back to the original loss of life and destruction of the world which relates to our original fall (Genesis 3—11). In principle our sins are the same as those that dragged the creation down. When we sin an individual sin, we are simply filling up the cup of all our fathers. This single massive network and narrative of sin is the sin for which Christ came to atone and in atoning he liberates the creation from sin and the curse!

The True Measure of Sin

The cross claims that the true measure of sin is not how we feel about it or how repulsed we are by it or even how much agony it has cost us when others have sinned against us. As I see it, this is one of the places at which the cross appears in its most scandalous light.

God does not hold us responsible for *not* being God. And when he teaches us (as he does throughout the Bible) that he sees sin more clearly than we do he does not hold us in contempt because that's true. He understands we *can't* know it as he does because no one is holy as he is holy and it is only the holy one who truly sees sin for what it is. So when we feel and speak against it as we do—limited though our sense of it is—he is pleased with the genuineness of our renunciation. *Just the same, he insists on our believing that the true and full measure of human sin is seen only in the cross of Christ.*

But see how difficult that is for millions to believe. Let me focus on the astonishing evil that exposed itself during the Hitler years. There must be a thousand books that rehearse the crimes that leave us speechless until we feel we *must* say something if only to keep from saying nothing. And who can forget the images that we've seen on television and in movies? Haven't we at times been on the verge of rising to stick our boot through the television set in irrational fury? And haven't we once or twice shouted at God, "How could you let this go on?" This is how we who are spectators feel, so how must it have been for those who were actually enduring it?

Now try telling those people that the true measure of sin is not the crucifixion of the Jews and other nations by the Nazis at Auschwitz, Dachau, Buchenwald, and elsewhere. Tell them that the true measure of sin is revealed in the crucifixion of a young Jew on a cross outside Jerusalem some 2,000 years ago. Tell them that and see their response!

Tell that to those who know what has happened in the gulag prison systems down the years where on Solzhenitsyn's conservative figure, 68.7 million people have died after prolonged crucifixions. Tell it to the multiplied millions who lived in the dark nights of Stalin, Papa Doc, Pol Pot, and numberless oppressors ancient and modern. Tell them that the New Testament teaches that the comparatively humane death of Jesus Christ is the true and full revelation of sin and evil's nature and together they will tell you that you're mad. And they'll feel insulted beyond measure because it will look like you're minimizing the awfulness of their loss and the twisted malevolent evils that confound adequate description.

But that's not what the New Testament is doing. That's not at all what the cross of Christ does! *It doesn't make less of all that—it makes more of it!* We see all that as moral evil and the cross says it's more than that—it's *sin!*

When my child is raped or my family tortured I want you to tell me that my feelings matter and that my pain is a measure of the sinfulness of sin. *But I want you to tell me it's worse than that!* I want you to tell me that *God* thinks it's worse than that. I want you to tell me that there aren't enough words in the entire world or enough passion in the whole of humanity to damn it with. When my personal pain is multiplied by tens of millions and we stand in speechless rage and utter bewilderment at the sights and sounds of it we want someone to say, "Yes, the eternal God agrees with you. It's as bad as you feel. Your devastation and your ceaseless fury-filled protests are a measure of it all. *But it's worse even than that.*"

That's what Christians mean to do when they say the cross of Christ is the true measure of sin. Minimize the world's hurt and the oppressor's wrong? God forbid! And the cross forbids! When Judas betrayed Christ that night something more profoundly serious had happened than a friend turning against a friend. A "world spirit" was defying eternal holiness. Spiritual hosts of wickedness were weighing in against holy love. Cosmic corruption and pollution was showing itself and coming to focus in that specific moral crime and in that specific person. That's what Luke meant when he said Satan entered Judas! At the cross it was more than religion and politics and racism in a deadly mix doing away with an innocent man (as they have so often done). It was sin against God himself. It was human evil as part of a corruption that reaches beyond the stars. The monster that swelled in the nineteen thirties and forties in Europe until it blocked out the sun is beyond our comprehension. As inexpressibly vile as these crimes are they are only the ulcers generated by a galactic predator that has ravaged worlds seen and unseen. Sin!

At Calvary, Christ was saying to every sufferer down the ages, "What has happened to you is more sinister than you know. It is part of creation's self-destruction; it's part of creation's sinful alienation from its God and you in your awful agony have exposed its hind quarters." But we could never have known this except via the cross of Christ for that is where the alien power fully exposed itself. We could stutter something legitimate about moral evil but we couldn't see it as "sinful" because the word "sin" only makes sense when God enters the picture.

Make less of our astonishing cruelty and inhumanity? No, Golgotha *is* Auschwitz and Africa and Cambodia and every other hell-hole seen through the eyes of God. We don't mean to diminish evil and savagery when we speak the cross. We have another agenda in mind. So while we pile up the phrases and pour out the rhetoric, we live out and speak out and act out—in our ordinances—the cross of God. We catch the sparks that fly from God's confrontation with Sin and our eyes are opened a little to what it is. Here's how Thomas Guthrie described it in his *Gospel in Ezekiel:*

> Look now at Sin; pluck off that painted mask, and turn upon her face the lamp of God's Word. We start, it reveals a death's head...It is a debt, a burden, a thief, a sickness, a leprosy, a plague, a poison, a serpent, a sting—everything that man hates it is; a load of curses and calamities beneath whose crushing, intolerable pressure, "the whole creation groaneth." Name the evil that springs not from this root—the crime that lies not at this door. Who is the hoary sexton that digs man a grave? Who is the painted temptress that steals his virtue? Who is the murderess that destroys his life? Who is the sorceress that first deceives and then damns his soul?—Sin. Who with icy breath, blights the fair blossoms of youth? Who breaks the hearts of parents? Who brings grey hairs with sorrow to the grave? Who...changes sweet children into vipers, tender mothers into monsters, and their fathers into worse than Herods—the murderers of their own innocents?—Sin. Who casts the apple of discord on

household hearts? Who lights the torch of war, and carries it blazing over happy lands? Who, by divisions in the Church, rends Christ's seamless robe?—Sin. Who is this Delilah that sings the Nazirite asleep, and delivers up the strength of God into the hands of the uncircumcised?…What Siren is this, who, seated on a rock by a deadly pool, smiles to deceive, sings to lure, kisses to betray, and flings her around our neck, to leap with us into perdition?—Sin. Who petrifies the soft and gentlest heart? Who hurls reason from her throne, and impels sinners, mad as Gadarene swine, down the precipice, into the lake of fire?—Sin. Who, having brought the criminal to the gallows, persuades him to refuse a pardon, and with his own insane hand to bar the door against the messenger of mercy? What witch of hell is it, that thus bewitches us?—Sin. Who nailed the Son of God to that bloody tree? And who, as if it were not a dove descending with the olive, but a vulture swooping down to devour the dying, vexes, grieves, thwarts, repels, drives off the Spirit of God? Who is it that makes man in his heart and habits baser than a beast; and him, who was once but little lower than an angel, but little better than a devil?—Sin. Oh! Sin. Thou hast insulted his holy Majesty; thou has bereaved him of beloved children; thou hast crucified the Son of his infinite love; thou has vexed his gracious Spirit; thou hast defied his power; thou has despised his grace; in the body and blood of Jesus, as if it were a common thing, thou hast trodden under foot his matchless mercy. Brethren, surely, the wonder of wonders is, that sin, is not that abominable thing which *we* also hate.

The Relational Nature of Sin

It can't be said too often that reconciliation is not a *legal* matter. It is not the restoration of a person to a *status* though to use such speech is legitimate. It is the restoration of a person to the Holy Father. And it can't be said too often that sin is not a *legal* matter even though it involves the breaking of what we sensibly and rightly call moral law. The moral law—despite biblical use of court and juridical metaphors—is the law of a *Father.* Since atonement deals with sin in order to restore a broken personal relationship we need to get the relational nature of sin clear in our minds.

It's right to insist that the Holy Father is a judge but it is never right to say that when he acts as judge he has ceased to be the Holy *Father.* God's judgement is real and his righteousness is as genuine as any earthly judge's but it is always a father dealing with his (wayward) children. God certainly punishes when he sees the need to do so but it is always a father dealing sternly and in holy love with his (wayward) children. And the man or woman who doesn't know the difference between how a judge functions as an officer of the court and how he is as a father at home needs to spend time either at court or at home or both. God didn't create mere "creatures". He created us as sons and daughters (Luke 3:21,38 and note Acts 17:24-29) so when we rebelled and "left home" it wasn't a court judge we were leaving or a code of ethics we were abandoning, it was our Father.

When we rebelled it wasn't a set of rules we turned against it was a holy Father. When we broke his commandment we broke his law and so in a sense we committed a "legal" crime but that isn't the real nature of it. *Sin is relational infidelity.* In scripture when he speaks to us in juridical terms and metaphors God isn't misleading us; he is using familiar categories to get through to us. He also expects us to get "the big picture". No father that we have any respect or affection for speaks of his child's misbehaviour at home as "breaking the law". It isn't "illegal"; it's something else, something that goes down to deeper roots. The child hasn't done wrong against a set of rules nor is she facing an officer of the court, a stranger who is somehow unrelated to her. This is her *father* for pity's sake! Family relationships are not to be reduced to "law abiding" connections.

What difference does it make if we see sin as legal or relational? It has profound ramifications for how we see the atonement and reconciliation. If sin is a legal matter then atonement must have a legal character and reconciliation also. Believing these things are legal issues, our atonement theory and the result of the atoning process is a legal process and a legal result. *Status* rather than relationship is what we talk about and *relationship* becomes a matter of book-keeping. Because juridical speech and metaphors have been given center stage for centuries it isn't surprising that our dominant atonement theory is legal to the core and retributive justice the primary motif in explaining the cross. Atonement is to reconcile and restore persons to a personal God and the way in which personal relationships are restored is by a relational atonement process.

Have we got rid of sin when we call it relational rather than legal? Why would we even think that? Does wrong committed against the family disappear because we won't call it "legal"? Are hearts and relationships less wounded because we deny that they are "juridical"? And in our fight against sin, do you think we'd fight harder against the betrayal of our beloved or the breaking of some law? Would we feel more or less remorse if we broke a law that mattered or broke a heart that mattered? Can we generate more passion to keep laws or to honor and serve the beloved? And anyway, how much do we care about a law that we think *doesn't* have the welfare of persons behind it? Our law will always remain only a law until it becomes the heart's desire of someone we're devoted to. Seeing sin (and righteousness) as *relational* will affect how we understand reconciliation and give added strength in our ongoing brawl with sin.

It's important that we see the other side of the coin. Righteousness is not conformity to a code of ethics though uprightness and moral rectitude are involved. Righteousness is relational fidelity. It is personal! It's the way people respond to their personal relationship with God. It has nothing to do with law-courts or legal status. Moral law has no independent existence though what we mean by "moral law" is profoundly real. But moral law has its source and shape in the personal Holy Father—it is a profile of God. However limited, it ultimately reveals God himself as he relates to his children and when we "obey the law" we are living in the image of God as his beloved children. And that's a million miles from courthouses and juridical categories.

Not Ashamed to Be Called Their Brother

"Christ bore our sins by fully
identifying with the human
family even while he fully
identified with the Holy Father."

The Heart of the Matter

The New Testament is crystal clear about this: Christ bore our sins on the cross! There are those who think this means that our sins were transferred to Christ and that God punished him with the punishment that was due us so that we won't be punished. Due to the fact that what Christ did on the cross was nothing but the will of the Father, it's crystal clear to me that God would not punish him during his holy obedience. But then, I don't believe that God *punishes* anyone that is innocent; therefore, he didn't punish Christ. Nor do I believe that guilt or the penalty for sin can be transferred to someone innocent.

The cross is indispensable to our salvation. It is Christ who alone saves us but it is "Christ crucified" that saves us. The issue is not can humanity be saved without the cross of Christ—of course it can't! Nor can we doubt that Jesus bore our sins because the New Testament says it over and over again. These truths are truths that we must continue to insist on. It just isn't good enough to say, "X amount of punishment was due our sins. Christ was punished with X amount of punishment so that God could forgive us." That theory of atonement is neither legal nor moral nor biblical. The best that can be said for it (and it's a lot) is that it takes sin and the cross of Christ seriously but it misses the heart of God and the true nature of atonement by a long way.

The Meaning of 'He Atoned For Sins'

Christ didn't come to condemn human sin as much as he came to atone for it and so condemning it was a step along the road to what he really wanted to achieve. He didn't come to condemn the world (John 3:17) but to save it from its sin by atoning for it. He knew what sin was, saw it better than anyone else, knew it needed atoned for and came to do that very thing. And he came to atone for it because he wanted to reconcile the world to his Holy Father. What does it mean that he "atoned" for it? *It means he so dealt with it that it could not keep God and his wayward children from coming together in the peace of reconciliation.* In the words of T.F. Torrance (which need development), "It means that the sinner's status *qua* sinner is rejected, and he is freely given the status of one who is pure and holy before God." And how did he atone for it? One of the ways the New Testament explains it is in terms of Christ "bearing" our sins. 1 Peter 2:24 says this, "He himself bore our sins in his body on the tree, so that we might die to sins and live for righteousness; by his wounds you have been healed." And Isaiah 53:11 closes with "and he shall bear their iniquities" (see also 53:12). What does it mean that he "bore our sins"? Among other things it must include the following.

In what way did Jesus "bear our sins"?

It means he put himself in harm's way to deal with our sin. In scripture when a person (or a nation) bore his own iniquity he took responsibility for it and faced the consequences. In the case of Jesus he made *our* sins his responsibility and faced the consequences of them *along with us* and on our behalf (I'm speaking of *identification with* rather than any legal transference of guilt). By the will of the Holy Father and the malicious spite of sinners he was made a curse for us (Galatians 3:13).

It means he took it upon himself to carry our sins to the place of judgement (the cross) where our sin could be dealt with. Only in the death of Jesus Christ—a death that was a glad and holy obedience to his Father's will—could sin be fully recognized and confessed to be what it was. Only in the holy and obedient death of Christ could the ultimate homage due to God's righteousness be given so that sin could be taken away because only in holy death was his holy life consummated. Only there *God* was getting what he deserved by way of unadulterated and loving obedience.

It means that he gladly "endured from sinners such hostility against himself" (Hebrews 12:2-3, RSV) as led to his death. Christ was no mere martyr and neither was he merely a hero. He gladly embraced death because it was the Holy Father's will rather than a self-chosen agenda. But the death the Holy Father purposed for him was death at the hands of sinners so that the true nature of sin might be unveiled. Ask, "How truly awful is sin?" and a minister of Christ will point to the cross and say, "That's the measure of its evil."

It means Christ became a sin offering. 2 Corinthians 5:21 reveals that "God made him who had no sin to be sin for us, so that in him we might become the righteousness of God." Christ wasn't literally turned into sin, of course. That speech makes no sense and the text doesn't say he was made "a sinner". The text says he who knew no sin was made to be "hamartias". This word is used repeatedly in the Greek Old Testament to mean the "sin offering" (see Leviticus 4:21,24; 5:12; 6:17; 10:7 and elsewhere along with Romans 8:3 where the RSV and the NIV use "offering for sin" in the footnote and text respectively).

2 Corinthians makes full use of Isaiah (and in fact goes on in chapter 6 to quote Isaiah 49:8 and 52:11) and this might tilt the scale in favor of rendering "sin" in 5:21 as "sin offering". In Isaiah 53:10 we're told that the Lord makes the servant "an offering for sin" (RSV) and that through him others are "made righteous" (53:11). On top of that we're told that the servant "did no sin" (53:9, quoted in 1 Peter 2:22). Let me summarize this.

In 2 Corinthians 5:21 he who had no sin was made sin and the result was righteousness for others.
In Isaiah 53:9-11 we have the servant who did no sin but was made a sin offering and made many righteous.

There is no need in any of these texts to think that bearing our sins speaks of "transferred guilt or sin". It won't do to think of Christ as a polluted sinner on the cross when it was precisely because *he* offered himself without spot through the eternal Spirit (Hebrews 9:14) that he could work atonement. Even the cry of dereliction ("My God, My God, why have you forsaken me?") implies his innocence for if he had been a sinner the answer would have been obvious. Besides it makes no biblical (or other) sense to hold one to be a sinner who was sinless in life and even more devoted to righteousness and holiness in his death. There is no sense in which God saw Jesus as a sinner because he was *always* with him because he did *always* the things that pleased the Holy Father (see John 8:29 and 16:32).

If the moral guilt of the world was transferred off them and on to Jesus Christ then the world would be sinless and Christ the only sinner. To say that the world's sins remained on the world but were transferred to Christ makes no sense. Besides, moral guilt is not transferable. We're not talking about electronic banking here with numbers in view; we're talking about relationships violated. And what's more, sin isn't just a wrong done, it's the pollution and contamination of a person. Conceptually the deed and the person are distinct but the deed has internal effects; the sinner's inner world is contaminated. It seems to me that talk of "transferring sins" only creates needless confusion. That Christ bore our sins and atoned for them is unequivocally true but these theories are a hindrance.

It is much easier to imagine Paul pointing to the Christ dying on the cross and saying, "There is sin being dealt with! There is sin being atoned for! In that person sin is being neutralized and in that person is the cure for our sin-disease!" If that's something like how we are to understand Christ being "made sin" then we can do without the talk of sins being transferred to Christ. (The related issue of Christ's personal righteousness being transferred to sinners creates more confusion and difficulty but it is part and parcel of this "transference" theorizing.)

Barth is helpful here (Volume 4/1 CD): "For the fact that God has given Himself in His Son to suffer the divine judgement on us men does not mean that it is not executed on us, but that it is executed on us...That Jesus died for us does not mean, therefore, that we do not have to die, but that we have died in and with Him; that as the people we were, we have been done away with and destroyed." (As quoted in Gunton, 111-112.) God doesn't make Christ *sin,* nor does he make him a *sinner* but in him he judges sin committed by sinners by bringing Jesus to death on a cross. There is no *transference* but there is total identification with sinners and in the judgement, "he bore our judgement" is proclaimed. Not apart from him! Not without him! In and through Jesus Christ sin is condemned and the sinner *as sinner* dies (see 2 Corinthians 5:15).

It seems to me that there's so much *pretence* in views that claim that God saw Christ as a sinner. We know Christ wasn't *really* a sinner but we must pretend he is to support our theory of how atonement works. We know Christ isn't *really* sin but we must pretend he is to explain our atonement theory. We know God wasn't *really* angry at Christ (even John Calvin thought the idea monstrous) but we must pretend he was in order to take sin seriously enough. The "cry of dereliction" gives us trouble when we try to explain it but we know in our bones (and in light of Acts 2:25-28 with John 8:29 with 16:32) that God didn't *really* abandon Jesus Christ. Especially since what he was doing was the Father's holy will ("not my will but yours be done").

And it doesn't help to see sin as meriting X amount of punishment, Christ bearing that amount and so saving those for whom he bore it. This kind of thinking harps on penal justice and ends up with a God who must, like Shakespeare's Shylock in *The Merchant of Venice,* have his "pound of flesh". It doesn't help much if we're reminded that he doesn't ask "a pound of flesh" from us but pays it himself. The fact is that in this atonement theory "the pound of flesh" must be provided. It seems to me if God can only forgive when the debt has been paid "to the uttermost penny" that there really is no true "forgiveness". Imagine a transgressor who has just served every day of his thirty-year sentence for his crime. He's finally released and society says to him, "We now graciously forgive you!" There's something unsettling about a God who can't forgive until the full measure of punishment is fully carried out. It leaves one with the impression that the Holy Father is really a divine legalist and something like a cosmic Jekkyl and Hyde—one side of him wants to forgive us and the other wants to sink us.

Even the word "satisfaction" (which is a perfectly good word) is generally used with the notion of "equivalence" or "the full measure" and that introduces the "pound of flesh" notion again. In Victor Hugo's *Les Miserables* the policeman Javert insists that all crime must be punished to the fullest extent of the law. In fact he commits suicide because in a moment of 'weakness' he had let a man off. In truth, of course, God is no Javert. Often though we're offered an atonement theory which seems to be more at home in an accountant's office or in the court of a judge who are perfect strangers and for whom the law is paramount. It makes you wonder. No doubt the Holy Father engages in judgement but it is a *father* who judges his *children.* To forget that is to distort fundamental truths and to forget the *relational* nature of sin and righteousness. It's all right, you understand, to say there are law-court metaphors and images in scripture applied to our relationship with God because "judging" is something God engages in but we're not to carry these images too far. God is *never* related to us exactly as a judge relates to the accused. He is always committed to us as a Holy Father is to his (wayward) children and it's pervasively expressed in terms of a covenant of grace. So judgement is never merely "justice" as over against "mercy" or "grace". Judgement is always an aspect of mercy and grace.

Furthermore, if we understand atonement as hinging on punishment administered how could the guilty *ever* be held accountable for their sins? If God took the innocent Christ and punished him with the full punishment due the world's sins it couldn't be right to administer further punishment. On top of that, it would be to despise the self-sacrifice of Christ and consider it insufficient. Would the world not say, "But the full punishment for all our sins fell on Christ and your wrath against our sin was exhausted"? Would they not say: "To punish us for sins that you have already exhaustively punished the Savior for makes light of his self-sacrifice"? I repeat, if the Christ is our substitute in the sense that we are now saying (that is, ours sins were credited to him and he was exhaustively punished in our place *and* his sinless personal righteousness was credited to us) how can we ever be punished? And what if it happens (as I believe to be true) that Christ bore the sins of the entire human race without exception, who could be lost if he has been punished with all the punishment due them? It isn't surprising that a "limited atonement" is closely connected with such an atonement theory. Those who believe in "limited atonement" think that Christ did not bear the sins of the entire human race but that he died for and bore the punishment of a select number. These (in consequence of that atonement view) can never be lost and their status with God consists of a forensic non-imputation of sin and a forensic imputation of Christ's personal righteousness. That doesn't work, biblically or morally.

In some ways it is misleading to think of how many people's sins Christ atoned for, whether some or all. It is *sin* he atoned for and therefore whoever is a sinner has a stake in the atonement. If he atoned for sin and there was a sinlessly holy person that person would have no stake in the atonement. The human family engaged in sin and Christ came to atone for sin and whoever is a sinner is offered reconciliation.

Christ bore our sins by fully identifying with the human family even while he fully identified with the Holy Father. He suffered *from* our sins. Not only did we physically abuse him we broke his heart by rejecting him. He suffered *from* our sins because he saw how we spurned the Father he adored and how we perverted the image of the Father who, in holy love, pursued us to restore us. He not only saw this but because his heart was his Father's heart he felt the pain his Father felt. He suffered *from* our sins because he saw us mutilate and betray one another and treat one another as if we were garbage. He raged and groaned at the sight of loss and injustice because he shared the love that the Holy Father had for the world. He suffered *from* our sins when he saw how we cheapened ourselves and fed ourselves on pig food, frittering away our days with trivia instead of living gloriously and fully. In all this and more he was *bearing our sins!*

Ezra & Christ Refusing to Distance Themselves From Sinners

He suffered *because* or *on account of* our sins because he refused to distance himself from us. He freely joined the sinful human family and was numbered with us. He entered into a family that was under the judgement of God because of its sins and he never stood apart from it professing he wasn't part of it. Romans 8:3 says he came not only in the likeness of flesh but in the likeness of "sinful" flesh. It wasn't a human family without sin he joined himself to but a family that was old in rebellion. When God called *the nation* to repentance and baptism for forgiveness of sins the Sinless One didn't excuse himself and claim executive privilege. One day John the Baptist looked up and there in line with sinners came the Son of God. John would have refused—how could Jesus have "needed" it?—but the Christ insisted in standing with his sinful brothers and sisters and responded to God's national call for repentance.

In Ezra 9:1-15 (RSV) we see this kind of thing illustrated in the righteous Ezra. The people are back at their wickedness, idolatry and treachery and Ezra hears of it. He's heartbroken and falls flat before God in a fit of repentance. Then rising to his knees he tears his clothes and apologizes to God because, as he says, "our iniquities have risen higher than our heads" (9:6). But Ezra was guilty of none of their crimes! Why then does he keep speaking of the sins as "ours"? Because he refuses to distance himself from his people. Even as the chapter closes we hear him saying (9:15), "O Lord the God of Israel, thou art just, for we are left a remnant...Behold we are before thee in our guilt, for none can stand before thee because of this." "Not one" of us can stand before God the righteous man said and he said that was true because of "our" guilt. Ezra saw their pathetic condition as part of the just judgement of God even though he himself had no part in that particular offence of which he spoke. So it was with the Christ who in utter holy righteousness identified himself with the sinful human family he chose to become part of.

We mustn't miss the point here. Ezra isn't overwhelmed simply because his brothers and sisters have sinned but because *he is part of a family that has sinned!* He doesn't see sin as something others have done all independent one of another. Their sin is his despite the fact that he was not in on it. His consciousness of guilt *in this particular case* is due to *identification* rather than personal sin. "We" have sinned against you!

Doctor MacLure came to see Annie Mitchell but there was nothing he could do for her, her life was ebbing away and the old man had to admit it. When her tongue-tied husband Tammas asked him if she was as bad as the doctor's face said, the old man could do no other than tell the truth. "A' wud gie onything tae say Annie hes a chance, but a' daurna; a' doot yir gaein' tae lose her, Tammas."

This hard-working, slow-witted man who always had difficulty expressing himself was so deeply in love with his Annie that the awful news was dismantling him there and then. There they were, the old doctor up on his horse, Tammas hiding his face in Jess's mane and the horse looking around at him as though she understood. His love made him a mouth and he said he wasn't prepared for this. "A' wes never worthy o' her, the bonniest, kindliest lass in the Glen...A' never cud mak oot hoo she ever lookit at me...She didna cast up tae me that a' wesna worthy o' her, no her, but aye she said, 'Yir ma ain gudeman...' We were mair nor man and wife, we were sweethearts a' the time...Oh, mah bonnie lass, what 'ill the bairnies and' me dae withoot ye, Annie?"

Margaret Howe stood by to comfort him but he turned to the doctor and pleaded, with a lost and desperate look on his face, "Can naethin' be dune, doctor? Can ye no think o' somethin' tae help Annie, and gie her back tae her man and bairnies?"

Margaret later said that their hearts were like water before Tammas' heartbreak and she saw the doctor tremble in the saddle as he bore the weight of the poor man's agony. It was then that she came to know how the loving old man identified with the people of the Glen. "A' never kent till that meenut hoo he hed a share in a'body's grief, an' carried the heaviest wech o' a' the Glen."

Christ bore our sins by becoming one of a family under God's judgement. In the previous section I made the point that Christ identified with a sinful family and here I want to stress that he identified with a family under actual judgement. Imagine a planet seething with rebellion and covered by a thunderstorm that represents God's judgement on that human family. The Word who was with God and was God chose to become part of that family that is under God's judgement and so he leaves heaven and enters into that storm. As part of that family he shares the judgement that rests on that family but it's a matter of *identification* and not *transference.* The judgement remains on the family even while the holy Christ shares that judgement with them. They aren't exempt from it. It never passes from them to him. In sharing the death they die he has no complaint though he hasn't earned their death. In his death on the cross he confesses in the name of humanity that God's judgements on sin are holy and righteous. The pain and loss he endures are *vicarious* as he shares the hurt that exists because his family has sinned. The pain and loss he endures are *representative* because he does it in our name as well as for our sake. In our name and as our representative he offers his holy obedience even unto death as the only fit homage that answers to God's holiness. In him (and only in him!) the whole human family is represented before God.

Hebrews 2:14-15 insists, "Since the children have flesh and blood, he too shared their humanity so that by his death he might destroy him who holds the power of death—that is, the devil—and free those who all their lives were held in slavery by their fear of death." His death rescues us and he expressly shared our humanity to share our judgement and as our representative defeat death and the Devil.

In all of this, there is no suggestion that our personal judgement, death, or sin are transferred off of us and on to Christ. He doesn't sin our sin but he is put to grief because of our sin. _He doesn't die a deserved death but he shares the deserved death that exists as part of the judgement on sinners._ The chastisement that brought our peace and reconciliation fell on him (Isaiah 53:5) because he insisted in joining us under God's judgement. Gary Williams in _Where Wrath & Mercy Meet_ (page 75) expressly denies that substitution allows for _sharing_ of judgement. He insists that "The sharing of punishment is not the same as substitution, since in substitution one goes free from the punishment and another suffers it for him."

Christ bore our sin by sharing the consequences of our sin. Matthew 8:16-17 may help us here. The text says,

> That evening they brought to him many who were possessed with demons; and he cast out the spirits with a word, and healed all who were sick. This was to fulfil what was spoken by the prophet Isaiah, "He took our infirmities and bore our diseases."

Matthew 9:1-8 insists on linking sin and disease. In it Christ insists on linking his authority to dismiss disease with his authority to dismiss sin. In 9:10-13 he defends his being with sinners on the grounds that they are sick and need a doctor (and he is that doctor). How does authority over disease prove authority over sin? The link is not "coercive force". It's not, "See I can exert coercive force to remove disease therefore I can forgive sins." The connection is moral and theological—in God's overarching purpose, disease and loss are part of God's judgement on sin (see below) and the removal of them connects with atonement, reconciliation and forgiveness. This is why Matthew links the healings with Isaiah 53. (And whose sicknesses did he bear? Matthew isn't saying that Christ bore only the sicknesses of *that* particular people on *that* specific occasion. He takes that occasion as typical. In all his healing sessions this was true. And was it only first century diseases he bore? No, he bore ours as well.)

Chapters 8 and 9 of Matthew are bracketed by the amazement of the crowds in 7:28-29 and the amazement of 9:33. In 7:28-29 it's astonishment about his teaching and in 9:33 it's amazement about his deeds. In between these we have the disciples amazed at his power over the elements (8:27) and the crowds at both his teaching and healing powers in 9:8. It's in that kind of a context that we find 8:16-17. Christ's authority (to which his words and deeds are witnesses) is marked and the people are astonished at it.

The fact that this section is clearly stressing the authority and power of the Christ and that Matthew connects Christ's power with his "taking" and "bearing" of their diseases suggests the nature of and grounds for kingdom authority. He has identified with the hurting and taken their sicknesses on his heart, to be his own, and so is empowered to remove them. *Kingdom authority and power is "bearing" and "carrying" power.* (And see 11:28-30 where Christ's "come!" is based on the fact that he is meek and lowly in heart.)

In all its essentials, Matthew follows the Hebrew text rather than the Greek Septuagint and has Christ bearing our *diseases* rather than our *sins.* As Christ healed diseases there is no suggestion that they were transferred from them to him. He doesn't become sick with their sicknesses or infirm with their infirmities and yet we're told he took and bore them.

There is something vicarious and redemptive here but there is no notion of *transference from them on to him.* Even in his dying (the ultimate expression of curse—Genesis 3:19) there is full identification with sinners but there is no transference of their death to him that makes them exempt from dying. *(If Christ can bear our sicknesses and diseases without transference maybe he can bear our sins without transference.)*

Matthew understands that the pains and losses in Isaiah 53 are the judgement of God on transgressors. Does this mean that every sickness is a specific judgement for some specific sin? No, because the innocent (babies, for example) and the righteous are diseased also. Besides there is John 9:1-3; and see below on Amos 4.

In Isaiah 52:13-53:12, someone was taking the nation's pain *as his own* and not simply removing it. Matthew must have viewed those healing sessions from a post-cross perspective and saw them as part of the whole atoning and reconciliation process. Sickness and death are part of the curse that God brought on humanity in response to our sin (see Genesis 3:16-19). *That curse was a redemptive move on God's part and was never intended to be a permanent situation.* Among other ways of looking at them, the miracles of Christ should be seen as promises and prophecies of the total removal of the curse (completed when death is obliterated—see 1 Corinthians 15:24-28). They are creative acts that bring light in the place of darkness, give life in the place of death and express sovereignty over the elements (like winds and waves). Whatever we think of that suggestion there is a definite bearing without "bearing *by transference*". Even when he takes his place on the cross and dies for us there is no suggestion that the death of all humans is transferred to him. He *identifies* with sinners and shares their experience of death and in this way he bears the consequences of their sins. But they aren't exempted from sickness and death, which would be the case if all sin and judgement on sin were transferred to Christ.

In Amos 4 (and in scores of texts like it) God seeks to redeem Israel and bring them peace by bringing them back to himself. To do that be brings drought and famine. If we suppose that a baby is born during a famine sent by God (as in Amos 4) it would suffer the effects of a famine *that exists as punishment for the guilt of an apostate Israel.* The child has done no evil (see Romans 9:13) but suffers from a famine that exists because Israel is evil and God wishes to bring them back to peace and the child's suffering arises from its solidarity with the nation. In this way the baby "bears the sins" of its national family (compare Exodus 20:5). The punishment that brought Israel peace fell on the child but God was not punishing the child! God did not "punish" the sinless Son though he certainly put him to grief and the chastisement that was to bring peace to the human family fell on him with wondrous results. There was no *transference* of Israel's sin to the innocent babies. The sinners remained sinners and the babies remained innocent though they "bore the sins" of their sinful human family.

He who "spared not his own Son" would not spare his own little children whose suffering and agony were a measure of Israel's guilt. But since the famine had a redemptive purpose (to bring Israel back to God we're told) the hurting babies were also a measure and revelation of God's relentless love as he pursued Israel's redemption. In a real way such a baby could say, "This is my body, which is given for you." In a profoundly fuller way Christ's choosing to be one with the family under judgement means he suffers the effects of that judgement though he is morally righteous and holy and not simply innocent as the babies in Amos' day. The suffering children cannot atone for sin; only Christ can do that! But the children of the world do us a redeeming service if we had the eyes to see it. And we're not to think that Jesus only felt compassion with the people he healed! *In identifying with the hurting he is identifying with sinful humanity that is under God's judgement. That is why Matthew links disease and sickness with the atoning work!*

In bearing our sins Christ saw us as sheep without a shepherd and he took our pain on his heart. The presence of physical suffering in the world is the proof of human rebellion but the Christ feels even the pain that comes to us in connection with sin. God anointed him with the Spirit to proclaim the glad message of freedom for the prisoners, sight for the blind and release for the oppressed. All this he saw in us and all this he came to redeem us from.

This is no "therapeutic nonsense"! In a multitude of 5,000 plus (Matthew 14:21) there must have been a lot of mixed motives, promises unkept, grudges harbored, self-serving, uncleanness and cruelty. Surely there was and if it was there Christ could see it for he knew people. And yet, when he looked, "he had compassion on them and healed their sick." (Matthew 14:14 and 9:36)

Tell me how can I be holy as he is holy? Help me to lift up my eyes and see better, purer, cleaner things. But help me to be holy like him and still look on people with all the marks of unholiness written on their faces and see them as needy people. What a wonder he is that he can look on the sinful and feel what they feel and long to do them good. There is a chasm fixed between us and Christ that we cannot bridge; his holiness simply outdistances our most fervent imaginings but is the chasm anywhere wider than it is at this point? It has nothing to do with miraculous power; it has nothing to do with his being able to feed thousands with little or nothing. It has all to do with his unutterable holiness looking on sinners and wanting to do them good, wanting to heal their sick, wanting to lift them out of their gloom and hurt and wanting to forgive their sins.

So there he stands looking at them with those big eyes of his. Missing nothing! Seeing all! And while knowing and seeing all he feels his huge heart swelling with pity at these sheep without a shepherd. So he healed their sick. I don't doubt that some there looked at him, fevered and crippled children in their arms, chins stuck out in some desperate look of rebellion: "How can you see us like this and not do something about it?" I'm sure others showed their desperation with "please" written all over them. There they were and here we are with our awful needs, stark and obvious to his holy eyes, masses of us clamouring for attention. People with little interest in him until our crying needs drive us out of ourselves and away from our useless schemes and shallow prayers. And still he looks and still he feels compassion and still he offers rich, wise, and desperately needed healing. Holy Christ! Astonishing Christ who makes it forever clear that true holiness isn't a firewall against fellowship; who makes it forever clear that true holiness is love's raging fire that burns down all that would come between his Holy Father and us.

The Blood-Stained Marcher From Edom

*"The cross made the resurrection
inevitable and the resurrection
proclaimed the cross as the
way to life and glory"*

Saving Justice from Bozrah

There is this terrific passage in Isaiah 63:1-6 where watchers see this figure striding with purpose and passion toward them and coming from Bozrah, the chief city of Edom. Edom, Israel's brother and cruel enemy. Edom who kept gouging when all others had grown tired. Edom, who joined the Babylonians forces against Jerusalem and timing their words, every time the huge battering rams hit the wall they'd chant "raze it, raze it, raze it to the ground." And who is the marcher coming from Edom wearing scarlet garments? So the watchers challenge him, "Who goes there?" and the answer comes back, "It is I, speaking in righteousness, mighty to save."

Not yet assured the watchers want to know, "Why are your garments red as if you had been trampling in the winepress?" The fast approaching marcher reveals himself as the Lord who had seen enough oppression of his people. He is pictured as hanging back, waiting to see if someone would put a stop to it but no one would so in his righteousness he deals with the enemy himself and his garments are covered with their blood as he works both retributive justice and redemption. Then follows praise and prayer and confession as the people remember their Lord who now in faithfulness comes to their rescue.

The Meaning of Righteousness and Justice

If you thought of a building when you heard the word "worship" what kind of building would it be? Almost certainly a synagogue, temple or mosque; certainly some building devoted to religious services. And if you thought of a building when you heard the word "justice" you'd probably think of a courthouse or some law-centered building. That makes sense because it's how we normally use the words. If you heard the word "righteous" or "righteousness" it would be a bit more difficult to connect it with a building because it has become a word essentially linked with morals and it's harder to connect that with a building. I think that makes it clear that in our Western climate the word "justice" and "righteousness" speak of two distinct realities that now and then connect. One is essentially *legal* and the other essentially *moral* and *religious.*

But the word "justice" is more than just legal, it usually (or at least *very* often) carries with it the notion of "getting what you deserve" and has the idea of punishment wrapped up in it. Seen in that light justice is not something we prize, it isn't something we'd plead for but something we'd rather not get. (We often hear this from religious people who will say something like, "When I'm before God I won't ask for justice because I want mercy. If I get justice I'll be condemned." That makes sense.)

But we use the word in another way. Oppressed people will often insist that what they want is *justice.* By this they mean something like fairness, decent and impartial treatment, and implied in this use of the word is the claim that they deserve to get equal or impartial treatment under the law. At least they're sure that getting that would be better than what they're getting. This has a solid Old Testament background where judges were repeatedly reminded that their business was to see that the poor and the marginalized were to get a fair treatment. This was stressed because for obvious reasons, the wealthy nearly always had the advantage over the poor. Nevertheless, the wealthy were to be treated impartially also and not to be penalized because they were blessed with wealth. Everyone was to get a square deal (justice) and that was determined on the basis of the covenant. The Hebrew noun *mishpat* would probably be the one best suited in this area since it covers the whole gamut of juridical and executive concerns. The Covenant Code or the *Book of the Covenant* (Exodus 21—23) is simply called *the mishpatim* in Hebrew.

Some Old Testament Texts

None of what follows is the least controversial. It is no more than a simple rehearsal of what you will find in any serious work dealing with the terms and the biblical use of them.

Justice is (often) the specific action God takes to respond to a particular situation. The Hebrew word from which it comes covers all kinds of "legal" type activities (Scholnick has shown us that in the book of Job it is a kingly/executive term as well as a juridical one). Righteousness is almost always used in connection with the covenant relationship he has with Israel. When we think of God "doing what is right" we need to remember that it is a relational word so that "doing what is right" = God keeping his word, being faithful to his covenant commitments. He makes a covenant (agreement) with Israel that he will be their King and Lord and so he will protect and bless them (see Isaiah 33:22). They agreed to commit to and serve only him with a glad-hearted allegiance and Moses calls this their "righteousness" (see Deuteronomy 6:22-25).

When God delivered Israel from her oppressors he was doing what he said he would do so his saving action = his righteousness. Look, when God was bringing down Nineveh it was salvation for Israel and punishment for Nineveh. God's righteousness and what we most often mean by "justice" (just retribution) come together in the single action by God. Presumably this is why the New Jerusalem Bible would render "righteousness" as "saving justice". And, listen, in giving Israel "justice" when she complained about Assyrian oppression didn't mean that Israel had *earned* anything by her moral excellence! She too was wicked (thus the national chastisement) but her covenant Lord vindicated her and rendered a verdict in her favor.

You often find other versions translating the Hebrew word for righteousness with words like "salvation" or "deliverance" or "saving deeds" (see the NRSV). And you find psalmists and prophets paralleling God's "righteousness" with his saving activity.

Psalm 71:15 has the psalmist saying, "My mouth will tell of your righteousness, of your salvation all day long." In Psalm 143:11b David says, "In your righteousness bring me out of trouble." In 51:14 we have "Save me from bloodguilt, O God, the God who saves me, and my tongue will sing of your righteousness." Isaiah 51:5-8 shows us that righteousness and deliverance and salvation can be used as equivalents. And there's Isaiah 56:1 where God says, "Maintain justice and do what is right, for my salvation is close at hand and my righteousness will soon be revealed." Psalm 98:2 sings out "The Lord has made his salvation known and revealed his righteousness to the nations."

When a psalmist prayed for "justice" he wasn't praying for some quality or other nor was he calmly admiring his moral excellence and asking God to treat him as he deserved. Almost always, he was in real trouble and he was asking God, who was his covenant Lord and partner, to fulfill the covenant commitments (compare Psalm 82 and see Isaiah 59:9,11 and 14).

Sometimes God chastised Israel but the chastening was also part of the covenant (read Psalm 89 :28-37). Punishment is provoked by Israel's faithlessness (unrighteousness). When God punished them, he was being faithful. Chastisement was a holy expression of his love (hesed—covenant love, and compare Revelation 3:19).

Covenant Righteousness But…

Though it's true that throughout the Old Testament God's righteousness is almost always used in connection with his covenant with Israel, there are some things we need to remember.

(1) *We need to remember* that before God made a covenant with *anybody* he was righteous. His righteousness is an aspect of his holiness and it is his *flawless moral character that leads him to act unceasingly in a way that is right.* But

since he is the source and shape of all that is right his righteousness is his self-consistency. He keeps faith with himself and because he is unceasingly true to himself he can never do anything that is other than right (compare Genesis 18:25 and Psalm 96 that speaks to the entire human race). So why does he do right by Israel—because he has a covenant with them? Yes, but the larger truth is that he maintains faith with Israel because he maintains faith with himself! God didn't begin to be righteous when he made a covenant with Israel at Sinai.

There are several words dealing with righteousness that give it a greater than "covenant" richness. There is holiness (qodesh), love (hesed), truth (emeth) and faithfulness (emunah). God's holiness is his essential nature, his transcendence above all else, his wholly "other" nature that is implicit in all his qualities and attributes. His holiness is seen in his righteousness and his justice. Isaiah 5:16 lays it out in plain language. "But the Lord Almighty will be exalted by his justice, and the holy God will show himself holy by his righteousness."

Love and righteousness (*hesed* and *tsedaqah*) are often paired together as companion qualities of God's action (Psalm 36:10). *Emeth* and *emunah* (truth and faithfulness) are from the same root and both stress stability and trustworthiness. We get our word "Amen" from *emunah* (see 2 Corinthians 1:18-21) and at least once the Greek Old Testament renders the Hebrew word for righteousness as "true" (Isaiah 41:26, rendered "right" in English versions). See the setting of Romans 3:3-7 with truth, faithfulness, righteousness and justice all in one breath. There's no reason to doubt that when Israel used these words they thought of them within the parameters of the covenant but the words burst the bounds of the covenant all over the place. See Jonah 4:2 where his love is for foreigners and Psalm 98:7-9 that tells us all the people should rejoice because God judges in righteousness. This should not lead us to deny that in the Old Testament, God's righteousness relates particularly to his covenant with Israel.

(2) We need to remember that prior to God making a commitment to Israel he had made a commitment to the whole of humanity (Genesis 3:14-15; 9:1-17 and 12:1-3 with the passages just mentioned). So we would expect his righteousness to be shown to the entire human family and not to be put on the shelf while he was dealing with Israel in particular. Again, this doesn't alter the fact that when his "righteousness" is mentioned it almost always relates to his covenant faithfulness to Israel.

(3) We need to remember that his covenant with Israel was one expression of his faithful outworking of his righteousness in relation to humanity. See this especially in Genesis 12:3, where in Abraham, all nations were to be blessed. God in redemptive faithfulness meant to bring the world together again in unity in one family of Abraham. That Abrahamic promise in Genesis 12:1-3 is in direct response to the fragmentation of the world talked about in Genesis 11:1-9. And Genesis 11:1-9 is the final phase of the record of the Fall which extends from 3:1 through 11:9.

That universal face of God's righteousness Israel forgot. If ever they had it they lost sight of it and became self-absorbed (though there are occasional voices raised against their elitism) so they went about to establish "their own" (Jewish) righteousness. Not only did they become self-absorbed they also became faithless and suffered the punishment of exile.

But they knew that though they were faithless, God would always be faithful. And that after judgement, he would bring them back to himself through and beyond the judgement (compare Deuteronomy 32:36-43 and Hosea 2 as illustrations).

The Glory of God's Righteousness In Christ

With the close of the Old Testament the Jews were expecting God to come to their rescue (see Luke 2:25 and 38 that speak of Simeon, Anna and others who were looking for the "consolation" of Israel and the "redemption" of Jerusalem). In the light of what we've just seen about God's righteousness we can rightly say that they were praying and hoping for God to reveal his righteousness (his saving justice) *toward Israel* in rescuing them from their enemies and their fallen state. They knew he was morally flawless but they were looking for a particular expression of his character—his redemption of Israel. *Be sure to see* Luke 1:67-79 and 2:25-32. That's what they looked for and what they got was Jesus Christ and the gospel of Jesus Christ.

The righteousness of God appeared in Christ crucified *and* it was independent of the Mosaic covenant *and* it embraced the whole human race! See Romans 1:16-17; 3:21-28.

As it worked out God's faithfulness (righteousness) was profoundly more wonderful than Israel could have imagined. The empire Israel wanted deliverance from was Rome but the empire Christ destroyed was vaster and more powerful than Rome. Rome was only one of the faces it wore (see the description of the Dragon and the Sea Beast in Revelation 12:3, 13:1 and 2b). The shackles that bound Israel were greater than social, economic and political chains—they were spiritual, religious and moral in addition to all the above. The inheritance the Messiah offered in light of the Abrahamic covenant was vaster than Canaan, it was the world (Romans 4:13 and also compare 1 Corinthians 3:21-23). And the resurrection he offered and personally initiated was not new life that would be subject to death again—it was resurrection to immortality, it was life that meant death was abolished.

In light of the Jewish expectation along with the texts from the gospels and the consistent Old Testament idea of God's righteousness, how should we view Romans 1:16-17 and 3:21-28? In light of the fact that God's righteousness was a *saving* righteousness it shouldn't be surprising to hear that the gospel is God's power *to save*.

Paul said (Romans 15:8-9) "Christ has become a servant of the Jews on behalf of God's truth, to confirm the promises made to the patriarchs so that the Gentiles may glorify God for his mercy." Christ is God's faithfulness publicly proclaimed to the world—he is God's righteousness and the gospel is the good news of his righteousness. In Romans that means, not the good news that he punishes sin (though that is good news) but, the good news that he has powerfully fulfilled and been faithful to his commitment to Israel and to the world. *We must allow that aspect of the cross to receive a fair hearing* and that means that we need to develop that truth before people. When they hear that God is righteous in Jesus Christ they need to be glad rather than sad and need to rejoice rather than be mortally afraid. Those who care nothing at all about the gospel and despise it have every reason to be mortally afraid.

The Public Display and Proof of God's Righteousness

In the Old Testament on the Day of Atonement the High Priest took the atoning sacrifice into the Holy of Holies, away from the eyes of the nation and there behind curtains he put away the sin of the nation with the blood of the offering. What God did in Jesus Christ was done openly (proetheto—3:25) and manifestly for all to see and he did it this way no doubt precisely because he wanted it to be seen. And he offered it as a proof or a demonstration (endeixin—3:26) of his righteousness. Does it matter to God that we believe he is righteous? It must or he wouldn't have gone to the trouble he went to. There was a time when Ezekiel saw in a vision what God was about to do to apostate Judah and it drove the prophet wild because he was sure it was overkill (9:8 and 11:13). But later, when speaking of the severe judgement on the apostates, God says to him (14:22-23), "Yet there will be some survivors...who will be brought out of it. They will come to you, and when you see their conduct and their actions, you will be consoled regarding the disaster I have brought upon Jerusalem—every disaster I have brought upon it. You will be consoled...for you will know that I have done nothing in it without cause."

I'm not suggesting that God sits on tenterhooks worrying about our opinion of him but more than once he was quite prepared to explain his actions to his creatures (compare Jeremiah 16:10-12; 22:8-9 and elsewhere). But it isn't at all unusual for people who believed that God was righteous to ask him for an explanation (Jeremiah 12:1) or to confess their confusion (Psalm 73:1-3). What they saw and experienced led them to ask how these things could be so and God remain righteous (that is, be just within the covenant parameters). This is part of what's going on in the book of Romans. Paul's gospel claimed Jesus was the Messiah, the Messiah had come to fulfil God's promises and yet the bulk of Israel was rejected. Paul's gospel claimed that the Messiah had to be crucified in order for Israel to be blessed, Israel slew him and is now rejected for it. They did God's will and have been cast off so how can that be righteous?

God's Righteousness and Passing Over Sins

The NIV of Romans 3:25b says God set Jesus forth as an atoning sacrifice and that "He did this to demonstrate his justice, because in his forbearance he had left the sins done beforehand unpunished." The NRSV says, "he had passed over the sins previously committed."

In this text it's clear that the cross not only saves us—*it saves God!* If the world in general and Israel in particular were as evil as Paul said they were in 1:18—3:20 how can it be that the holy God didn't utterly obliterate it? If Paul had told the truth about humanity's sin then God must have been soft on sin all those centuries. As Godet would have it, there existed a "four thousand year scandal." It would appear from the text that whatever else we aren't sure about we can be sure that sin wasn't adequately dealt with until God dealt with it in Jesus and the cross. It isn't necessary to adopt a penal substitution theory of atonement to see that in the text. It isn't necessary to claim that Christ had to bear the full quota of punishment for sin if forgiveness were to be made possible. It's clearly Paul's point that God's righteousness was not proved in this ultimate sense until the cross of Christ.

The translation of *paresis* as "left unpunished" doesn't make sense to me in light of the Old Testament record that tells us about the flood, Sodom and Gomorrah, the Korah rebellion and the exile. I don't see how "pass over" makes a lot of sense in light of Noah's flood or Romans 1:24,26,28.

It appears to be true that the word *paresis* is a weak word to use if Paul was speaking of forgiveness but it *can* be used for the remission (of taxes, 1 Maccabees 11:34) and the verb form for the remission of debts and other obligations (Arndt & Gingrich, 626). So maybe he intends to say sins were "remitted" (as in the KJV) but uses a weaker word for the process.

But why would he choose a weaker word and avoid the stronger words (*aphesis* and *aphiemi)?* Maybe he did it *not* to deny full remission in the Old Testament but to stress that the atoning sacrifices by which forgiveness was gained were only provisional and shadowy. The Hebrew writer who knew full well that forgiveness was gained via atonement in the Old Testament still insisted in 10:4 that the blood of animals couldn't take away sin. And despite the fact that we're expressly told repeatedly that if ancient worshipers offered sacrifices "their sins shall be forgiven" (Leviticus 4:14-15,20,26,31,35; 5:5,10 as examples from many) the Hebrew writer still says (9:15) that *Christ's* sacrifice redeemed from transgressions that were under the first covenant. So while forgiveness was genuine (compare Romans 4:7) and it was mediated most often by sacrifices (Hebrews 9:18-22) there was still a sense that sin had not adequately been dealt with via the sacrificial system. Maybe this is why Paul used the weaker word, to *suggest* this rather than develop it. He contrasted the openness of Christ's sacrifice as over against the hiddenness of the Yom Kippur sacrifices. Perhaps he's also contrasting the fully satisfying atoning sacrifice via Christ as over against the provisional means in the Old Testament. If this has merit then he could be saying that the pre-Christ sacrifices dealt with sin but didn't fully deal with them though they mediated forgiveness to the worshipers.

It's vital that we remember that no punishment of sins can possibly reveal in fullness the righteousness of God. Retribution is only one "weapon" in God's armory in his all-out war against sin. His full purpose is redemption and salvation and not simply punishment.

Buddhism and Hinduism protest against the doctrine of forgiveness as proclaimed by the New Testament. They believe that their doctrine of *Karma,* with its punishments throughout a series of lifetimes is more just because every wrong is paid for in pain or loss. No doubt that this is one way of taking sin seriously, which is more than the happy pagans of the world are presently prepared to do. But it might be that precisely because it *does* take sin seriously that it is the more dangerous to the full truth. When people simply dismiss wickedness we have little patience with their views and we are all the more tempted to accept a serious view of it as the full truth. Everything less than the cross is a tragic underestimation of sin. Is God soft on sin? And is his forgiveness immoral and demoralizing? It would be, said William Temple, if all he said about our crass wickedness and cruelty was, "Oh never mind; come along; let us still be friends." If that were the case, Temple goes on to say, "we could no longer worship Him. He would be below the level of our consciences. But no one who has received his pardon from the lips of Christ on the Cross is going to think that God says 'Never mind,' or that He does not Himself mind. That is how he minds." *(Christian Faith and Life, page 77)*

He would even be soft on sin if he simply punished us. This is what I mean. There are aspects of sin that cannot be brought out simply by punishment—punishment can't get to the bottom of it. Haven't we seen evil that absolutely beggared description and even when the transgressor paid with his life we knew that this didn't measure the depth of the evil he engaged in? That's what I mean. Only in the cross is sin taken utterly *seriously*.

And if we insist—as we should—that the cross is the primary place where God exposes the awfulness of sin maybe we'd spend less time whimpering about our sins. There's certainly a place for our repentance and sorrow for sin but that is no substitute for shining the light of the cross on it. Our ceaseless going on about how we've sinned is not the measure of it though it sometimes appears that that's what we think. It appears that we think that if we don't go on and on about it that we aren't taking it seriously enough. But we're too good at deceiving ourselves. The way to truly come to terms with the true and awful sinfulness of our sins is to delve into the unfathomable richness of the cross rather than look at how pained *our* hearts are. Those of us who are more guilt-ridden than others (or more self-righteous than others) tend to think that *we* are the ones who take sin most seriously. But it is not in us to assess sin for the depths of its ugliness nor are our hearts the place to look if we want to see sin for the ultimate abomination that it is.

The Universal Scope of God's Righteousness

Who is it that God in righteousness redeemed? How do we recognize them? Their God is God and they have Abraham as their father. Ah, then it's the Jews because they alone have the flesh of Abraham and God is their God. No, it's those who have the faith of Abraham with whom God made a covenant before he was circumcised (4:9-11). And what was the meaning and nature of Abraham's faith? He trusted in and committed himself to the God who could give life to the dead (4:17-22) and those who, in and through Christ believe the same thing are accounted as righteous (4:23-25).

Paul argues on the basis of monotheism (3:29-30) that the whole world is to benefit from God's righteousness. Three times a day the Jew devotedly repeated the Shema as a central and driving force of their faith and Paul makes a use of it many of them would never have dreamed of. If the nation went to its knees to confess the truth that there was one God then there was only one human family and God was committed to them all.

So what is good about the good news? The good news is that the whole world is under the oppressor Sin and that God couldn't and wouldn't tolerate it so he came to the rescue. The sin problem of 1:18-3:20 couldn't be dealt with by the torah (written or unwritten—2:12-15 and 8:3) but praise God it could be and was dealt with by Christ and his cross.

The good news is that through the torah, written and unwritten, God drove home to man throughout human history that if they were to be redeemed and have life it would have to come from him (see Romans 11:32).

The good news is that in the final analysis God doesn't focus on sin he focuses on life! He saw our faithlessness and because he had committed himself to us he could not leave us in our galactic ditch but in righteousness came to bind up our wounds, heal our sinful hearts and pour in the oil of the Spirit. Our hope and assurance rest solidly and secure in his "saving justice".

But God's "saving justice" implies the presence of sin and all that goes with it and it implies his judgement on it (in whatever form that judgement takes). His "justice" says he will not tolerate it, that he will not allow it to go on so he steps in and "does what is right." But he steps in to do what is right *in order to save!* And he steps in to save us *from what?* From sin and all that it brings.

And how does he do that? As Kasemann said in a 1961 lecture, "God's power reaches for the world, and the world's salvation consists in the fact that it is led back under God's dominion."

According to the will of God, Christ gave himself for our sins to deliver us from this present evil age (Galatians 1:3-4). God "has rescued us from the dominion of darkness and brought us into the kingdom of the Son he loves" (Colossians 1:13). That's how God saves the world. He brings them under one head, Jesus Christ (Ephesians 1:10) in whom God comes in righteousness, in saving justice.

The Power of God's Righteousness

God's righteousness is not just his *faithfulness,* it is his *saving* faithfulness. Paul said he was unashamed of the gospel because it was God's *power to save* (Romans 1:16). The gospel is the proclamation of God's saving deeds in Jesus Christ it is God's power to save. This is no salvation by education or knowledge as so many schools of philosophy offered and still offer.

Bultmann was absolutely correct when he said, "God's forgiveness is not deduced from an idea of God or His grace, but is experienced as His act in the event of salvation, so that preaching does not consist in illuminating instruction regarding the idea of God but in the proclamation of the act of God." And the gospel is God's power to save us by redeeming us because in it, God's *act* in Christ reveals his saving justice.

Yes, but does it really save? Yes, the cross of Christ is the world's salvation and the resurrection is the definitive proof that God has defeated the most powerful lord of all the lords. Romans 4:25 says Christ was offered up for our sins and raised for our justification (and see 1 Peter 3:21-22). The cross made the resurrection inevitable (see Acts 2:24) and the resurrection proclaimed the cross as the way to life and glory (Ephesians 1:19-23 and Colossians 1:18).

But arising out of the death and resurrection of Jesus Christ is the individual and corporate faith of the church, the witness to the world of the saving justice of God in Jesus Christ that will be brought to a glorious completion on a coming day. That faith, the ordinances and liturgy of the church, are signs of the *saving* nature of God's righteousness.

The faith of any individual in Jesus Christ is astonishing. We take its existence too much for granted. We tend not to think much about it, of course, but when we do many of us take it as almost "natural" that we believe. "Well, of course, we believe, what's the surprise in that, isn't Christ worth believing in?" Yes, of course he is worth believing in but it isn't the worthiness of Christ that I'm amazed at. What astonishes me is that people who have been shaped for so long by sin, living in a world that is really lord Sin's empire—it astonishes me that they have stopped believing in Sin and now believe in Jesus Christ.

We stress the truth that there is no faith in Christ without a free commitment to him as if that explained the existence of our faith. Look, it's precisely because we were blessed with free will that we became sinners in the first place. Free will is required if we're to have faith but free will doesn't explain *the existence* of faith in Christ. How does it come that we freely believed in him when the world was/is all-encompassing? How did we ever get free from it? Did we free ourselves by our moral strength? Did we face lord Sin, denounce and renounce him out of the moral and spiritual strength that we had without God? You understand I'm not talking about intellectual capacity at this moment, I'm talking about the amazing truth that at some point we turned to emperor Sin, defied him and walked away from him to Jesus Christ! That's called *repentance.* How did that come about?

It came about because God, in Christ crucified, came in saving justice and defeated lord Sin and then came in the gospel and told us he had done it. If he had not done that there would be no faith in Jesus Christ on earth. And the faith of every believer and the corporate faith of the church demonstrated in her ordinances of baptism and the Supper make the triumph of Jesus Christ over Sin and the powers visible and concrete. The grand biblical truth shows itself in actual individuals and congregations. So the believer should rejoice in his or her personal deliverance from sin's dominion but, additionally, they should rejoice because they are witnesses to something vast, something cosmic. They are witnesses to the glory of the crucified, risen and reigning Lord Jesus Christ. Isn't that amazing?

If we proclaim the gospel that Jesus is Lord and Savior and someone should ask us for proof of it we would of course turn to scripture. But it would be perfectly legitimate to point out the fact that we ourselves have faith in Jesus Christ and *that* is proof that the gospel is God's *saving power* because we ourselves have been saved by faith. He conquered our sin in bringing us to faith!

As long as the world stands there's a man who will be known as "the penitent thief" whose faith climbed over every conceivable obstacle to breathe free. Despite his background, his own agony, the appearance of the one dying across from him that said he was nothing more than a criminal like himself he said, "Lord, remember me when you come into your kingdom." This faith wasn't born in a soft home and comfortable circumstances and it was more than a personal commitment of faith. That personal faith was a proof that there, on that other stake, the world and all the principalities and powers were being stripped of their power and dignity (Colossians 2:15) by God's saving righteousness.

When a boy, a mere twelve-year old boy, leads his first public prayer he carries out a world-defying act! For all his nervousness and for all the quavering of his voice when he closes with that familiar "in the name of Jesus Christ" the whole framework of the satanic world trembles. And when a tiny congregation sings its praises to God in the name of Christ, the defeat and final doom of all that is anti-God and anti-life is pronounced. *These are proofs that Sin has been defeated and damned and all because of the saving righteousness Of God!*

So This Is Love?

*"And can the love of God
be a cool and wholly
dispassionate affair if he showed
it to us in Jesus Christ?"*

The Reality and Warmth of God's Love Toward Us

How can we be astonished at the love of God for us unless the word "love" has some true meaning even for us? Yes, of course there are differences between God's love for us and ours at its best for one another—differences that beggar description. But how is it possible for us to rejoice in the truth that he loves us if the word has no real meaning? If there is nothing in God's "love" that makes contact with what we mean by love when we use the word? If we came to believe that God's "love" for us was nothing but a clinical and coldly holy non-aggression could we rejoice in it? Could we be moved by it to devoted and heartfelt service? Would we be driven by the truth of it to costly self-sacrifice? Would we be able to stay with him when our sin jeeringly confronted us and scorned us with the claim that a glorious God would have no time for the likes of us?

The answer to all these questions clearly is no. If God's love were nothing more than an unfeeling decision not to destroy us it might give us some relief but it would bring us no joy. It would bring us no inspiration to do lovely and selfless things; we'd have to find our inspiration for that in other places than the love of God (but see 1 John 3:16b). Can you imagine that being true—anywhere near the truth?

And can the love of God *be* cool and wholly dispassionate if he showed it to us in Jesus Christ? Whatever the love of God is over there "in the land of the Trinity," when he showed it to us within the realm of humanity it became Jesus Christ. And does the love of God in Christ look like a cold, holy and clinically dispassionate affair?

The Loving Warmth of God's Holiness

We think of his holiness as a somber and isolated quality that makes him unapproachable. That sort of thinking, of course would make it difficult for us to believe his love could have warmth and affection in it. But what if his holiness isn't like that at all? What if his holiness is a passionate love so pure and so "other-seeking" that it desperately longs to make the beloved good? And what if it rages up in that holy passion in the midst of destructive evil, burning it to ashes? What if holiness *in God* is only another face of his love and what if his sin-hating love is only another name for his holiness that has redemption at its heart? And what if, in our sinful limits and our shallow love that wants to burn sinners who rise against us, what if we're allowing our sin and our shallowness to redefine *holiness?* What if, because of these, we see holiness as an anger that rages rather than a redeeming love that rages? What if, because we're sinful and we hunger to isolate transgressors, that we justify that hunger by calling it justice, which we link with holiness? And what if, in our sinfulness, we're recreating God in our own image?

Holiness: Its Indispensability and Nature

More than anyone I've read, Peter Taylor Forsyth stressed the holiness of God's love. The truth is, Forsyth made holiness the bedrock and made love an aspect of God's holiness. Maybe that's too subtle. But there's no doubt that in our present Western religious climate, we drown in sugar and syrup. While it is crucial that we say "God is love" it may be even more appropriate to say "the Holy God is love."

But I can't help thinking that we've narrowed the word "holy". We've made it equivalent to ethical purity. So that when we say God is holy, we mean nothing more than he is infinitely pure and righteous (and he certainly is!). But there's more to it than that! His "holiness" means that he is *beyond* all. Higher, grander, more majestic and glorious than we can imagine, so that his holiness is his *transcendence* rather than any one quality in or of him. He is *different* and *separated* from all else. And *that* is what the scriptures mean when it says he is "the Holy One". In Exodus 15:11 God is holy in contrast to all the gods. "Who among the gods is like you, O Lord? Who is like you—majestic in holiness, awesome in glory, working wonders?" And then there's Isaiah 40:25 that issues the challenge, "To whom will you compare me? Or who is my equal?" says the Holy One. He is different and above all else not because of any single quality in him but because he is what he is—in totality!

I've no wish to deny what the Bible plainly insists on, that God's holiness has an ethical quality that means he reacts in hostility to all that is evil (be sure to see Habakkuk 1:13). It's because that's true that he is so different from the sinful human family and different from all the ancient and modern gods that practice or are indifferent to wickedness. It shouldn't surprise us then that, when dealing with hardened sinners, the ethical purity of his "holiness" is the issue that is stressed. God is actively hostile to sin and experiences holy recoil against it.

(Mark you, God's recoil against sin isn't a "reaction" in the sense of an unthinking and reflex action. A corpse will react and jerk when an electrical current is shot through it. No, all that God is he is because it is his will to be so. As I earlier mentioned, God doesn't just "happen" to be holy and loving. He is a "person" and *lives* rather than merely exists and in living he chooses as a dynamic, personal being chooses. And because he is what he is, his choices are ceaselessly and effortlessly righteous and pure.)

So when we say God is holy we're not to think *merely* that he is ethically pure and opposed to all that's evil, we're to think that he is glorious beyond our wildest imagining. *He is different!* But one of the truths and realities about God that makes him infinitely different and greater than us is his love! *In that respect his love is part of what it means that God is the Holy One!*

We shouldn't want God to be all sweetness and sugar. Because we are what we are—sinners at a profound level—in our lucid moments we should want God to take sin seriously, even if they're ours. And whatever our views of the atonement, however we think the cross fits into our redemption, the cross of Christ makes it clear that God takes sin seriously. There's no waltzing around the entire tone of scripture that God hates sin with an unchanging and unbending hatred. So it gets in the way between us and him and he will not tolerate it. His holy love moves him to deal with it because it is contrary to his nature and because it would destroy any hope we have for fullness of life with him.

God Explaining What Love Really Is

So we should have peace and believe 1 John 3:16 when it says, "This is how we know what love is: Jesus Christ laid down his life for us." Yes, we should see to it that our understanding of the word "love" is shaped and enriched by the biblical witness but we shouldn't be afraid of being loved by God. And then we're told (4:9-10) "This is how God showed his love among us: He sent his one and only Son into the world that we might live through him...and sent his Son as an atoning sacrifice for our sins."

You would think John was ignorant of all that the Old Testament revealed about the love of God, but not a bit of it! He knew the Old Testament very well but he also knew that something astonishing, something almost incredible had taken place in the coming and the dying of Jesus Christ. I'll tell you what's incredible; it's incredible how we can hear such good news and think it quite understandable. It's perfectly clear that there's more than one reason why we can receive such truths with a minimum of difficulty but one of them, surely, is that we've become accustomed to it. That can't be avoided I suppose. But maybe if we spent a bit more time listening to the Bible speak to us rather filling our minds and mouths with religious chatter, we might tend less frequently to take such truths for granted. Listen to Paul's passionate outburst in Romans 5:6-8 as Peterson (in his careful though expanded version) gives it in The Message.

> Christ arrives right on time to make this happen. He didn't and doesn't, wait for us to get ready. He presented himself for this

sacrificial death when we were far too weak and rebellious to do anything to get ourselves ready. And even if we hadn't been weak, we wouldn't have known what to do anyway. We can understand someone dying for a person worth dying for, and we can understand how someone good and noble could inspire us to selfless sacrifice. But God put his love on the line for us by offering his Son in sacrificial death while we were of no use whatever to him.

At which some non-believers wisely and knowingly nod. They're unimpressed—there's nothing new here. With a little bit of humanity and some plain commonsense wouldn't we all come up with such observations? In truth, haven't we always known this? Haven't we all known what? That God has felt this way about us? What crass nonsense that is. John says we wouldn't recognize the love of God if he hadn't made it known in Jesus Christ. Scots theologian of some years ago, Hugh Mackintosh, said we talk almost glibly of the loving Fatherhood of God as if it were as equally obvious as the claim that grass is green. It is no such thing! And besides, the love that is seen in the giving of Jesus Christ is more than general warmth and affection.

The death of Christ is not just an act of dying—it is a redeeming death, an atoning and sacrificial death. Who knew that until the Bible spoke and who knew that to its depths until God spoke in and as Jesus Christ? Mackintosh said that this conviction "rose like a new planet over the world's horizon at a definite point in history." It took the revelation of the cross to open man's eyes to what God's love is toward us and as a consequence, to the fathomless depths of the life that is to be ours when God completes the enterprise.

So we mustn't cheapen the love of God and bring it down to this paltry level where every sentimental act of ours is supposed to illustrate the love God has for us! This addiction to making our little children smile by catering to their every lisping wish reflects neither the Old Testament or the New Testament teaching about God's love. It just "thrills" us to see their little eyes light up when they ask for even "more" and we "can't help" giving it to them. And with that I must hurry to say that the love we have for little children is something precious, something we should thank God for and should make known in daily practice. What I'm anxious to avoid is this sugary indulgence that falsely goes under the name of "love". It's hard for us sinners, but the attempt must be made by God's grace, to tell the difference between love and its counterfeits. Wherever "love" becomes more concerned for our happiness than our holiness alarm bells are ringing. Without the cross at the center of it or even the thought of the cross at the center of it "love" can become "a self-centered devouring passion, bent only on extracting from its relationship the maximum of personal delight, without care for the needs or wishes of the object beloved."

But it would be very wrong to think that a cruciform love finds no pleasure in loving or in the beloved, far from it! Christ speaks about the joy of God in Luke 15, a joy that finds that the return of sinners is something to celebrate. It's a fitting occasion to throw a party and to dance as old Laclan Campbell did when Flora came home.

Ian Maclaren in his lovely book *Beside the Bonnie Brier Bush* echoes the heart of the gospel when he tells us what happened at Drumtochty. Drumtochty! A little tight-knit community isolated from the world in the hills of Scotland; where the deeply pious and stern old Lachlan Campbell lived with his twenty year old daughter Flora. Campbell loved her deeply but didn't have enough of whatever it takes to speak freely of it; didn't have enough vision or whatever it takes to know that lovers must speak and the loved ones must hear; didn't have the breadth of understanding to know that life needs joy as well as other basic things.

The heartsick man came to the church leadership to announce that his "worldly" child had run away to the wicked world of London. He asked that her name be stricken from the church record as he, driven by strict principles, had struck her from the family Bible. A pathetic letter from Flora said:

"Dear father,—When this reaches you I will be in London, and not worthy to cross your door. Do not be always angry with me, and try to forgive me, for you will not be troubled any more by my dancing or dressing. Do not think that I will be blaming you, for you have been a good father to me...but it is not easy for a man to understand a girl. Oh, if I had only my mother, then she would have understood me...Forget poor Flora's foolishness, but you will not forget her, and maybe you will still pray for me...When I think there will be no one to look after you, and have the fire burning for you on winter nights, I will be rising to come back. But it is too late, too late. Oh, the disgrace I will be bringing on you in the glen.

Your unworthy daughter,

Flora Campbell."

The whole village knew what Marget Howe knew about Lachlan. While he babbled on about the weather and things, his eyes were all the time saying, "Flora, Flora". Marget, who had also suffered a great loss in the death of her beloved son, George went to Lachlan's house to see him.

When he showed her the wavering strokes in the massive family Bible that scored out Flora's name, she was furious. "This is what you have done, and you let a woman see your work! You're an old man, and in great pain, but I'm telling you before God *you* have the greater shame. Just twenty years of age this spring, and her mother dead. No woman to watch over her, and she wandered from the fold and all you can do is to take her out of your Bible!" she blazed at him.

Lachlan blazed back at her but eventually calmed down and blurted out his grief-filled admission of wrong, lapsing into Gaelic, none of which Marget understood, though she did make out Flora's name and another that she took to be Flora's mother. She wrote a lovely letter to London telling the girl how her father was wearing out his heart for the sight of her and that she was to come home immediately.

Flora started home right away. But how to board the train with so many Drumtochty locals on it? She didn't have the heart for it. Peter Bruce the station master, spotted her in the shadows and spoke kindly to her: "Ach, lassie, I didn't recognize you at first, but I heard you had been visiting in the south." With some excuse that "third" class was packed full he slipped her into a better compartment in "second" and found reasons to keep others from wandering into it. On arrival he told Flora to wait for a moment, and sprinted to his nearby house to tell his wife the "Cammil" girl was coming. Mary greeted her with such warmth, not a word about her wanderings; even *thanked* her for coming into their home on the spur of the moment and "without ceremony".

When she finally arrived at her own familiar hills in the dark, worry seized her, because she knew full well her father's iron principles. But she need not have worried, for when she turned a path that led to her cottage the kitchen window was a blaze of light, welcoming her home. A lamp, sitting on several theological volumes and the huge family Bible, beamed out the heart's desire of a lonely father who missed his away-from-home daughter. As she came near the dogs inside the house started yelping with delight, sensing her approach, and she could hear her father feeling for the latch, so eagerly that he had difficulty finding it, and he was saying nothing but, "Flora, Flora."

Later, she rehearsed to Marget her awful loneliness in crowded London, "and when I looked in at the lighted windows the people were all sitting around the table, but there was no place for me. Millions and millions of people, and not one to say 'Flora,' and not one sore heart if I died that night." But that was past and with a heart bursting with joy, she said to Marget, "It's a pity you don't have the Gaelic. It is the best of all languages for loving. There are fifty words for darling, and my father was calling me every one that night I came home."

I don't know *who* warms me more in this lovely story. The old man whose lifelong hardness is dissolved by love into confession and change? Marget Howe's brave compassion that reached out in love to both father and daughter? Or Flora's joyful eagerness to return and make amends, coupled with her ecstasy at being loved.

I don't know what warms me more. The old man's using fierce theological volumes and the accusing Bible to set the lighted lamp of "welcome home" on, the villagers helping Flora on her way home or the fact that any language has fifty words for "darling"?

Learning to Rely On and Trust In God's Love

We love such stories not only because they are beautiful but also because they are true to life as even we sinners know; they are believable. They're within our reach and they draw us. But I think it's precisely this that makes the cross indispensable as a revelation. Why is it that the sensitive people need so much assurance about the love of God? Isn't part of the answer because God is infinitely pure and holy and that our guilt makes his love for us close to unbelievable? If God were not so pure and holy, if we had not learned that from the scriptures in general and Jesus in particular, maybe we could have received his love with less persuasion. "Of course he loves us, and why wouldn't he? What's not to love?" But he is that pure, that righteous and that holy and our guilt haunts us. Our sinful and wavering hearts cry out for assurance and where is it to be found? It's to be found where John says it is to be found. "This is how God showed his love among us: He sent his one and only Son into the world that we might live through him."

But just to be sure that we get the message he lays it all out again in 1 John 4:14-16. Here it is in J.B. Phillips' version. "We ourselves are eye-witnesses able and willing to testify to the fact that the Father did send the Son to save the world...So have we come to know and trust the love God has for us."

John uses two perfect tenses in the verse sixteen. Somewhere in the past they had come to know and come to trust the love God has for them and even as he writes they know and trust it still. And what is it based on? It's based on the fact that the Father did send his Son to save the world. Phillips renders the word pepisteukamen (from pistueou—

believe) as "trust". The NIV gives "rely on" which is close to the same thing but adds a little richness to the truth. Just to let the sound of it run over the mind lifts the heart. "The Father sent his Son and this is how we have come to know and rely on and trust in the love God has for us."

It may well be that Glasgow preacher W.M. Clow was right, we will never truly believe in the love of God until that day when we find ourselves home in a better world and all fear is gone. Poor sinners that we are. Still, maybe (maybe!) if we reflect on the cross of Jesus Christ we'll get some rich sense of it even now. At least that is what George Herbert wanted for us and worked toward in his poetry. If you like religious poetry you may not like George Herbert's work but if you love it you will devour his material. He has two poems listed as Love and here's one of them.

Love bade me welcome; yet my soul drew back,
    Guiltie of dust and sinne.
But quick-ey'd Love, observing me grow slack
    From my first entrance in,
Drew nearer to me, sweetly questioning
    If I lacked anything.

'A guest,' I answer'd, 'worthy to be here':
    Love said, 'You shall be he.'
'I, the unkind, ungrateful? Ah, my dear,
    I cannot look on Thee.'
Love took my hand, and smiling did reply,
    'Who made the eyes but I?'

'Truth, Lord; but I have marr'd them; let my shame
    Go where it doth deserve.'

'And know you not,' says Love, 'Who bore the blame?'
    'My dear, then I will serve.'
'You must sit down,' says Love, 'and taste my meat.'
    So I did sit and eat.

Paul's point in Romans 5:6-8 that God sent his Son to die for us when we cared nothing for him as a result of both our rebellion and the consequent weakness it created in us, is confirmed by John. In 1 John 4:10 he insists, "This is love: not that we loved God, but that he loved us." And then in 4:10: "We love because he first loved us." There's something sinfully tragic about our inability to accept this constant stress in scripture that God has made all the running in our relationship with him. Paul asked a church that swaggered and swelled because of its rich blessings (1 Corinthians 4:7), "What do you have that wasn't given to you?" We don't have to buy his favor—he gives freely!

It isn't necessary that we earn his love or that we do enough to make sure he will continue to love us (read Herbert's poem again). There are some who might think it is necessary for us to sweat and strain to gain God's favor but that was never true. Paul makes it clear in Romans 10:6-7 that it isn't necessary for us to coax Christ into coming to save us nor is it necessary for us to generate the power to make him alive from the dead. If it were required of us to do any of this we'd be eternally in trouble for we're not up to it.

J.R. Seeley, whose view of Christ and the Christian faith was less than the New Testament proclaims, in his book *Natural Religion,* page 173, tells of an interesting conversation between Talleyrand and Larevelliere-Lepaux.

Paris born Alexandre Talleyrand was a Catholic high churchman and statesman during the years of the French Revolution. Larevelliere-Lepaux was a member of the Revolutionary Directory, a philanthropist and a passionate critic of Christianity. The philanthropist tried to improve matters by establishing his own version of deistic "Christianity" but was terribly disappointed that it was making no progress. "His propaganda made no way," he said; "what was he to do?" he asked. The ex-bishop politely condoled with him, feared it was indeed a difficult task to found a new religion, more difficult than could be imagined, so difficult that he hardly knew what to advise! "Still,"—so he went on after a moment's reflection—"there is one plan which you might at least try; I should recommend you to be crucified and to rise again the third day." Seeley remarked, "Yes indeed! This is a lightning-flash that clears the air." And so it is.

We're not able! But the New Testament everywhere says that He is able! More than able, eager and already involved, already doing for us in holy love what we could never do for ourselves. Loving us before we loved him and in his holy love of us drawing us back to himself.

We need to note that it is Jesus who laid down his life for us. We need to note that it is God who sent his Son, that it was God who sent his Son, that it was God who sent his Son as an atoning sacrifice for ours sins and that it was God who sent his Son not to destroy us but that through him we might live.

"This is how we know what love is: Jesus Christ laid down his life for us."

"This is how God showed his love among us: He sent his one and only Son into the world that we might live through him...and sent his Son as an atoning sacrifice for our sins.

An Eternal Crisis in the Life of God

"…because he is an infinitely holy lover of his creation, obliteration was only a theoretical possibility and the suffering of God was inevitable."

The Cross and God's Eternal Commitment

The cross of Christ was not a new way for God to relate to his creation. The historical cross was the revelation that God *cannot* relate to a fallen world in any other way. This is why Peter says Christ was ordained before the world began (1 Peter 1:19) and why John said Christ was the Lamb that was slain from the foundation of the world (Revelation 13:8).

Paul insisted that God's purpose and grace was given to us in Christ Jesus before time began, but that it was only *now revealed* through the appearance of Christ as Savior (2 Timothy 1:9). I don't doubt that there is the element of purpose in the text (it says so!) but I think we need to remember that *purpose* takes its rise from the nature and character of God. He wills and purposes according to his heart and that heart was *revealed* in its fullness in Jesus Christ. The cross is an historical revelation of God's unchanging character and commitment to his creation.

My suspicion is that God initiated atoning sacrifice among humans as a reflection of his own relationship with fallen humanity. Human rebellion created "a crisis" in the life of God. To obliterate humanity was a theoretical possibility because God is infinitely holy, but because he is an infinitely holy *lover* of his creation, obliteration was only a theoretical possibility and the suffering of God was inevitable. (The agony of godly and loving parents in the face of the extreme waywardness of their beloved children would illustrate my point.) So when humans offered atoning sacrifice—sacrifice provided and regulated by God—they were expressing the divine situation that would come to its ultimate unveiling in the Lamb that was slain from the foundation of the world.

The inevitability of God's suffering isn't some "deep structure" necessity that was imposed on God by something external to himself. It is an eternally free choice by God. But it is an eternally free choice that is inevitable because of his nature and character and commitment to the creation. (I say a free choice because God *lives* rather than merely exists. He doesn't just "happen" to be a holy lover, his holiness and love is his *will*. A block of ice doesn't "will" to be cold. God eternally wills to be holy and loving.) His will to suffer with and from and for sinful humans because he has a holy faithful heart finally expressed itself in the cross that atones for the world's great wrongs and offers boundless life. But how does Christ's sacrifice work? How did sacrifice work in the Old Testament?

Old Testament Sacrifices and Offerings

The remarks that follow relate to sacrifices and offerings almost exclusively from an atoning angle and that has real dangers. Not only does it miss the great variety of offerings expressly mentioned in scripture but it also tends to see nothing but *sin.* One of my own weaknesses down the years and one of the weaknesses (so I presently judge) of evangelical literature and preaching is the extremes we run to. At one end of the spectrum God is all sweetness and sugar and on the other he ceaselessly rages about the sinfulness of the children he has fathered (see Acts 17:25-29). If he were a human father of the kind we preach not only would we not admire him we would be profoundly disappointed in him. We'd worry about his mental health!

My defense for sticking mainly to the notion of atonement is that there is more implied in atoning sacrifices than appears on the surface. They are not preoccupied with sin and much less, the God who initiated them is not obsessed with sin and his own reputation.

Everyone is sure that the Old Testament sacrifices worked atonement and brought forgiveness because there are scores of texts that say just that (Leviticus chapters 4 & 5 illustrate). But exactly how they functioned in bringing that about has been debated for years and the debate still rages. I suppose it's like every other profoundly rich topic, it has so many angles that we find it bewildering. With truths like this it's easier to say what *isn't* true than it is to get anything like the whole truth about it. Still, there are some proposals that are obvious enough and it makes sense that we should begin there.

Sacrifice Was God's Idea and Not Man's

This is true at least of the Mosaic sacrifices. Offering sacrifices didn't begin with the Mosaic covenant but Leviticus 17:11 is rightly taken as a text that speaks for the whole sacrificial system under the Old Covenant. "For the life of a creature is in the blood, and I have given it to you to make atonement for yourselves on the altar; it is the blood that makes atonement for one's life." In saying, "I have given" the blood it seems clear that God is stressing the purpose he is assigning to the shedding of the blood (atonement) but it's nevertheless true that he is the provider of the sacrifice since the flocks and herds come from him. Leviticus 17:11 makes it clear that there's no magic involved in the atonement and that there's no magical power in the blood. This giving of the life by shedding the blood of the sacrifice for atonement is the express will of God and nothing other.

I'm going to assume what some scholars for good reasons dispute: from the beginning, atoning sacrifice was initiated by God. I think Genesis 3:21 implies that the cover for the human rebels required the life of some animal and we're told that it was God rather than the sinning pair that provided the cover.

It's clear that man didn't come up with the idea of atoning sacrifices because man doesn't take sin seriously enough to think such a thing is warranted. Nor would man even have seen his sin in so serious a light if God had not revealed it to him.

God Initiated the Sacrificial System as an Expression of His Holy Love and Grace

Atoning sacrifice did not rise from humans who were trying to placate God who threatened to destroy them every time they sinned. The sacrifices were not ways in which the sinners bought mercy and grace from the Holy Father. The whole enterprise was an exercise of God's holy grace that enabled them to live with one for whom sin is the one unendurable. It "covered" (or, following Richard Averbeck, it wiped away) their sins. The gracious and inexpressibly generous nature of the sacrificial arrangement was beyond our poor grudging and stingy hearts and if we know anything about real sacrifice and generosity we learned it from God.

There's a way to view the sacrificial system that gives the impression that God is ceaselessly musing about sin and how it needs to be punished but this entirely misses the point. The God who initiated the atoning arrangement had a whole different agenda in mind. The people to whom he gave this way to peace and life were already thoroughly sinful and yet God went to their rescue. In Exodus 19:4 and 20:2 God describes himself as their deliverer who brought them, not to mount Sinai, but to himself. He wanted them and it didn't seem to matter that they didn't want him, it was enough that he wanted them and that was the driving force behind his rescue operation that brought them to a life-bringing relationship with himself (and see John 1:10-11). So when he initiates the atoning system he is not obsessed with sin at all, he is fulfilling the covenant he made with their fathers because he loved them (see Deuteronomy 7:7-10 and 9:4-6).

It is wearisome to read the ceaseless harping on the wrath of God though there's no doubt in my mind that an aspect of sacrifice was to deal with the sin that would become an occasion for the wrath of God if it were not dealt with. Some write about sacrifice averting the wrath of God and leave the impression that God is forever scowling at his sinning children, always on the verge of striking them a blow with his almighty fist. What does it matter if every now and then they remind us that God is gracious if every other page is filled with "proof" that God's wrath is about to burst forth if the sinner doesn't sprint to the tabernacle or temple with an atoning sacrifice?

It just isn't true that God forever sits trembling in holy recoil at sins committed as if he can barely hold his wrath in check. If godly parents looked or behaved like that we'd be appalled. And in light of their hair-triggered judging style their acts of kindness wouldn't offer us a lot of assurance or peace because we might think the kindness was out of character. When we portray God as obsessed with sin and punishment it doesn't really help people if we cite some verses that say God is slow to anger and is filled with loving-kindness.

Sacrifice Was Initiated By God to Work Atonement

Old Testament sacrifices and offerings had more to them than atonement as we can see by the various kinds of sacrifices spoken of in the biblical text (see also the literature on this matter). Behind all the peace, thank, votive and free-will offerings we must remember that they all take for granted that the worshipers have access to God. For sinners, that requires atonement and forgiveness. There is something to forgive and while it might not trouble us a great deal it certainly troubles God!

Leviticus 4 & 5 repeatedly tell us that sacrifices (animals or products of the earth) work atonement and that forgiveness of sins is part of that *at-one-ment* between God and his child. I think it is correct to say that God is propitiated by the atoning sacrifice but we do need to be careful how we say such things because it's too easy to generate an image of God as a supersensitive Father recoiling at the very sight of sin. Words like satisfy, appease and propitiate can too easily mislead. That sacrifice "satisfies" God is clear but in what way does it satisfy God? Maybe we try to explain too much rather than to thankfully receive the surface truth. This much is clear. The sin, if not dealt with, jeopardizes the relationship the child or the nation or the world has or could have with God. When the sacrifice is offered and is acceptable to God, he is satisfied that the sin has been dealt with in such a way that he forgives without compromising his holiness or de-moralizing the sinner.

Bearing in mind that the sacrifice is nothing without the penitent hearts of the worshipers, the atoning sacrifice dealt with the sin that could result in the outpouring of God's judicial hostility (see Deuteronomy 7:10, Exodus 32:9-10 and elsewhere). But the picture is not that the sinner sins, God immediately gets mad, rises to his feet with a bowl of wrath at the ready and only resumes his place with a satisfied smile when the sinner offers the sacrifice. God knows that sins are inevitable (compare Matthew 18:7, Luke 17:1 and 1 Corinthians 11:19). And when Christ taught his disciples to pray, he took it for granted that they indeed would sin and would be in need of forgiveness (Matthew 6:12).

This is a complex matter and a few phrases aren't really very helpful but we say some things to keep from saying nothing, don't we? Wrath is outpoured when sin is not atoned (include both repentance and sacrifice in that process) so, in effect, God initiates and provides the atoning process so that he will not need to punish. If punishment takes place it is precisely because the sin has not been dealt with. Atonement is not an implicit threat, as if to say that God is forever warning them that he could just crush them for their sin—it's a provision and offer of forgiveness despite sin! The difference I'm suggesting is a difference of attitude and emphasis. There are those of us who seem to want to stress the wrath that could be poured out rather than the grace that is being poured out.

Just reflect for a moment on the tone Christ must have had when he said he came to give his life a ransom for many (Matthew 20:28). Of course there is the existent danger implicit in the fact that they need rescued but he is not at all suggesting that they need to be bought from God! The whole atoning process acknowledges the danger that sin (impenitent sin) puts the sinner in but, its very essence is generous rescue. Atonement is a rescuing, saving, redeeming business!

Sacrifice Called For the Worshiper's Heart

For atonement purposes God did not accept the sinner without his sacrifice but neither did he accept the sacrifice without the sinner. The enlightened and sensitive worshiper knew that there was nothing mechanical or merely external in the offering of sacrifices. David was never slow to offer sacrifices but he and others like him fully understood that what God wanted was the worshiper's heart and loving obedience. Here's what he said in Psalm 40:6-8

Sacrifice and offering you did not desire, but my ears you have pierced; burnt offerings and sin offerings you did not require. Then I said, "Here I am, I have come—it is written about me in the scroll. I desire to do your will, O my God; your law is within my heart."

In Psalm 50 the psalmist speaks the heart of God in the words of 7-14 where he says God doesn't feed on animals and if he did he would not depend on Israel to offer them to him. It would appear that at some point the people weren't offering sacrifice and God said that that wasn't bothering him (50:8—he'd seen plenty of those). What he wanted from them as sacrifices were loving gratitude and faithfulness that would lead them to keep their word (50:14,23). And in Psalm 51 with the Bathsheba and Uriah affair in the background, David knows that what God wants is inner truth (51:6), a pure heart and a steadfast spirit (51:10). Then in 51:16-17 he acknowledges that God does not "delight in sacrifice" or "take pleasure in burnt offerings" but that "the sacrifices of God are a broken spirit; a broken and contrite heart."

It should come as no surprise to us that it was well known that if sacrifices did not represent the heart of the offerer, they were worse than nothing. God had made it clear to Saul, the king he had chosen and then deposed, that it was obedience he wanted and would not accept sacrifice (no matter how impressive) as a substitute for that humble obedience (see 1 Samuel 15:13-23).

God makes that truth clear to us from another angle. How many texts can you remember (even if vaguely) where God rebuked his people for their heartless offerings? There isn't any need to quote a lot of them because a couple (from among many) makes the point clear. "The multitude of your sacrifices—what are they to me?...I have more than enough burnt offerings, of rams and fattened animals; I have no pleasure in the blood of bulls and lambs and goats...Stop bringing meaningless offerings." (Isaiah 1:10-11,13) And why was he sick of them, why were they "meaningless"? Because they were substitutes for the total reality that God truly wanted. He wanted the sacrifice to be an expression of the sinner's repentant heart. (Where sacrifice was provided and called for it was required even from a good heart!) They offered him animals and he said, "Your hands are full of blood; wash and makes yourselves clean. Take your evil deeds out of my sight! Stop doing wrong, learn to do right! Seek justice, encourage the oppressed. Defend the cause of the fatherless, plead the cause of the widow" (Isaiah 1:15-17, and compare the sustained exposure of externalism in chapter 58). And in 66:2-3 there is this blunt, scathing indictment of a heartless people who brought their animals. "This is the one I esteem: he who is humble and contrite in spirit, and trembles at my word. But whoever sacrifices a bull is like one who kills a man, and whoever offers a lamb, like one who breaks a dog's neck; whoever makes a grain offering is like one who presents pig's blood, and whoever burns memorial incense, like one who worships an idol." (In light of all this wouldn't you think that people who describe Old Testament worship as "merely ceremonial" should read a little more in the Old Testament scriptures?)

An Atoning Sacrifice Wasn't "Punished"

It is true that in the case of an animal sacrifice that the sacrifice died and there is reason to believe that God's judicial wrath is averted but neither of these truths are equal to the proposal that the sacrifice was *punished.* It is one thing to *suffer* for someone else and another to be punished "for" someone else. One is an everyday experience in life and a common occurrence in scripture but there's no such thing as being punished for someone else. It is expressly forbidden in scripture and it is clearly immoral as well as illegal. The idea of God *punishing* the innocent is outrageous though it is true that God may put the righteous and the innocent to grief for the benefit of others.

It is clear that the offering is identified with the sinner that offers it (assuming the sinner means it to be so). This we can see in the whole atoning procedure. The transgressor confesses the need, brings the unblemished animal *leans on* it (not simply lays hands on it) fully identifying himself with the offering, and slays it. It seems clear in all this that the sacrifice in some sense becomes a sin-bearer. All that is clear enough but there is nothing about transference of sin, nothing about the animal being punished and nothing about it suggests that the *sacrifice* displeases God or that it comes under his wrath as if God thought it guilty.

But if the sacrifice is a sin-bearer does that not mean that sin has been transferred? No, not at all! See pages 114 – 119 for a discussion of Matthew 8:16-17 where Christ bore the diseases of people he cured and there was no transference of their diseases to him. See there also for a few remarks on Isaiah 53:5, which says that chastisement that brings us peace fell on him.

Besides, in this whole atoning process it isn't only the animal that bears the iniquity of the sinner—the priests are expressly said to bear the iniquity of the people. See Leviticus 10:17 and Numbers 18:1. The NIV obscures the Hebrew text and renders the same phrase in two different ways in those two texts. See the other versions. What those texts show is that the priests bear the iniquity of the people and for the holy things and for the priesthood. That covers everyone and everything. No one as far as I know suggests that the sins are transferred to the priests. Transference isn't in the picture.

Both texts are "bearing" texts but they clearly mean that the priests functioned to make atonement so that the sins were forgiven rather than that the guilt was somehow credited to them.

And when the scapegoat is sent off into the wilderness outside the camp it to becomes a sin-bearer and a *national* sin-bearer since it is part of the Yom-Kippur ritual. Again, there is no transference of sin or punishment suggested. *The animal, as a living picture, carries Israel's sin outside the camp of the nation into the wilderness and so declares that all the sin in Israel has been taken away.* All this is possible because the people and the individuals fully identify with the atoning ritual and make a heartfelt confession of the sin that needs to be removed. In all this a case can be made for the averting of God's wrath or at least for dealing with sin (which if not dealt with would be an occasion for God's wrath). There is at no point any need to talk of sins transferred or punishment of the innocent. Neither is there any textual justification for it. To say that atoning sacrifice averts the wrath of God is one thing but to say it averts the wrath of God by bearing punishment is another. One is no doubt true but the second is not supported by the texts used to support it. It is illegal, immoral and contrary to God's word to punish the innocent (see Deuteronomy 24:16)! It simply isn't enough to say sacrifice averts God's wrath *as if that in itself* proved in what way the sacrifice averted his wrath!

Some Truths Underlined in Atoning Sacrifices

God initiated the sacrificial system to show that he took their sins seriously and the sinner offered the sacrifice because he agreed with God that his sin was indeed serious.

God initiated the sacrificial system so that sinful Israel could continue to have life in covenant union with him and Israel offered the sacrifices because they wanted life with God in covenant union to continue.

God initiated the sacrificial system to give Israel a way to confess that they hadn't given to God what was fitting for God—unswerving obedience. When God said he desired mercy and not sacrifice (Hosea 6:6) he was not dismissing the offering of sacrifices because the sacrificial system was *his* idea. It served a purpose that a generally lovely life could not accomplish. A devoted life was nevertheless not without sin and even the holy people confessed that they too were sinful and in need of sacrifice. Their sacrificial lives were not spotless nor were they in totality offered up to God, but when they offered the sacrifice they were offering to God in spirit what they were unable to fulfil in execution.

God initiated the sacrificial system because he fully understood Israel's sinful limitations and the inevitability of their sin against him and their ceaseless need of forgiving grace.

God initiated the sacrificial system to assure Israel that their sins were truly taken away and that they were in good standing with their sovereign Lord. In coming to God with the heart he calls for in the way he prescribed, meant the sinner could know that despite his or her sins they were at peace with God. This had its risks as well as its assurances but God was willing to take the chance. (Haven't we met people that we thought were "too assured" on the grounds that they had once been baptized into Christ's death? At times we might even have thought *we are them.*)

God initiated the sacrificial system to instruct Israel that they must take him seriously. God made that truth very clear in Malachi 1:6-14 when responding to their sacrifices. They were offering the sick and the feeble from a wicked heart and God asks them if they would give such offerings to their governor. He concludes in 1:14 with this trenchant warning. "Cursed is the cheat who has an acceptable male in his flock and vows to give it, but then sacrifices a blemished animal to the Lord. For I am a great king, say the Lord Almighty, and my name is to be feared among the nations." God is no vain, peevish and petulant sovereign. He is the Lord Almighty and he is a great king! He is not only worthy of honor he insists on being honored. This insistence is not only because he has the right and because he is worth it, but it is of vital importance that we know and acknowledge that. As soon as a puny little man thinks there is no one higher or greater than him he sinks even lower than he is. A great family or cause or nation calls us up higher—so does a great King!

God initiated the sacrificial system so that Israel would know that salvation began, was maintained and would be completed by a gracious God!

God did not initiate the sacrificial system to make it easier for Israel to sin or to give Israel reason to believe that he thought sin was no serious matter.

God did not initiate the sacrificial system to exempt Israel from glad-hearted and holy obedience or to teach Israel that sacrifice was a substitute for such obedience.

God did not initiate the sacrificial system so that Israel could purchase grace from him or placate him into being gracious or forgiving. He was already and eternally that way.

God did not initiate the sacrificial system to teach that obedience was completely *unrelated* to reconciliation.

The New Testament and Christ's Sacrifice

"Christ loved us and gave himself up for us as a fragrant offering and sacrifice to God." That's what Ephesians 5:2 tells us. Hebrews 7:27 says of Christ that "He sacrificed for their sins once for all when he offered himself" and in 9:28 we're told "so Christ was sacrificed once to take away the sins of many people." In 1 Peter 2:24 Peter says "He himself bore our sins in his body on the cross" (NIV). He uses the word *anenegken,* which is the usual word in the Greek Old Testament for offering sacrifice and which means to carry *up* (the altar was raised—see its use earlier in 2:5). Christ bore our sins *up* on to the tree (the Greek text has the word for tree rather than cross) as on to an altar so that as we look at the stake on which he died it becomes an altar of sacrifice.

In light of the New Testament very few indeed would take the view that the death of Christ was not essential to our salvation. The (sometimes) clashing theories of atonement all agree that without him and his cross-work we would be lost. The bulk of the argument is about how to express that truth and clearly, some ways of saying it are simply not true. While some theories are just not true, it's more often the case that theories are true but they tell only a part of the truth. It's astonishing how quickly my favorite theory becomes the only theory.

If you read through the material above on Old Testament sacrifices and thought it useful you might want then to look at the sacrifice of Christ in light of those proposals and remarks. If you add to that the earlier efforts to say things about the cross of Christ that didn't immediately have an atoning thrust then you'll excuse the brevity of this summary.

The cross of Christ means nothing of an eternal nature without taking into account who he is, his life as a whole and what he meant to do with it. In Psalm 50 God said he wasn't into eating animals and the idea that he has some special delight in blood-letting misses the truth by light-years. God is not a God of death or sin or sickness. He is a Holy Father whose driving concern is holy, joy-filled *life* in fellowship with his creation. He deals with sin and works through suffering and death, but these are not his preoccupation! The cross of Christ is about life, about redemption and the coming glorious completion of God's purpose in a glorified humanity reigning with Christ over a liberated creation with the curse removed and sin and death completely obliterated.

It seems clear to me that the notions of satisfaction and substitution are aspects of the atoning work of Christ. It seems to me that when God has dealt with sin in and through Jesus Christ that his holy self is content that the human race can be freely and fully forgiven without their being de-moralized and without God compromising his holiness. And it's evident that Christ stands to represent the human family and to do for them what they could not do for themselves and it's certainly the case that he became one of us and bore our sins (but without the silly notion of transference of sin, guilt and punishment).

But his cross was grander than a mere means to avert our punishment. It dealt with more than the penalty for past sins for it was and is the power to recreate us. Averting wrath is not nearly enough, it is holy communion with the Holy Father we need if we are to *live* and Christ went to the cross to gain that for us (2 Corinthians 5:15 and 1 Peter 2:24). To sunder salvation from sanctification is to deny the truth of these two passages, which expressly tell us that he died "so that" we would die to sin. These texts are not saying that since he saved us we should reciprocate and live like him. They explicitly say that the purpose of the cross was to bring about our death to sin and our life unto God. Salvation and reconciliation *is* sanctification!

The cross of Christ served all the purposes outlined in the comments above on Old Testament sacrifices. Of course it is profoundly more comprehensive and in many ways too obvious to list how his sacrifice differs from them (see the book of Hebrews).

In the cross, Jesus not only died *in* the flesh, he died to it. "The flesh" stands for many things in the New Testament but it certainly stands for all that is weak and creaturely that has set itself up against God and suffered loss as a consequence. In Jesus Christ, God's judgement was rendered on "the flesh", but not in a rush of savage spite or sulking pride at being sinned against. He judged it in Jesus Christ that he might recreate it and raise it to glory, honor and incorruption. The way of the cross, for those who are embraced in the redeeming work of Christ, is the way of life—rich, brimming, glorious life!

A Careless Rage For Life

"Jesus Christ swore that
he had come to see that people
would no more be robbed but that
they would have life to the full!"

Doers and Dreamers

Every now and then you come across someone, either in literature or personal experience, who strikes you as having a greater appetite for life than all others you have met.

Alexander the Great seems to have been like that. Filled with plans, eager to get on with them and glowing with excitement and energy as he went about them. At twelve he rides a horse no one can ride. At sixteen he leads his own punitive divisions against Illyria and saves his father's life at Chaeroneia when Athenian crack troops were about to overwhelm him. He couldn't untie the Ghordian knot so he hacks it to pieces and he wades chest deep in water sometimes up to eight hours to get an advantage over an enemy. He insists on fighting a lion single-handed and using only a knife. He'd jump off his speeding chariot just to see if he could catch it again and he would scale the walls of a besieged town, risking his life inside the walls while his men were trying to break down the gate. Poor soul, in some ways he was too high strung and he died at thirty-three, but in that brief time he took great gulps of life and *lived!*

The English novelist and playwright Dorothy Sayers, it seems, was of a similar bent though her great gulps of life were not quite Alexandrian. She once described herself as someone who had "a careless rage for life." We need such people, don't you think? Not wasters but dreamers, and more than dreamers, doers. And there are others, like Van Gogh, restless for more life and, yes, too high strung.

And then there was and is Jesus Christ. No fever, but fervently filled with life that was brim full of life. Jesus Christ who swore that he had come to see that people would no more be robbed but that they would have *life to the full!*

It can't be said too often that the life Christ brings to us is really *a relationship.* But how can life *be* a relationship? Of course it can, try making friendship something other than the relationship. The life he brings is a relationship that has two phases. One is here and now and the other is the completed gift in a better world. And yet, the gift of life he brings is never completed because we go on living and growing into his likeness here and hereafter. Both phases are ours only in and because of our relationship with him. Never apart from him! Never independent of him! Never! At no point! Ever! Not ever!

The present phase of that relationship includes forgiveness, a new status as part of a new creation and life transformation even while we live in a fallen and dangerous world. It also involves moral war, disappointment, suffering and death. The second phase is the continuation and consummation of the present. It means we personally and individually experience the redemption of our bodies in a glorious resurrection to share his likeness and reign with him over a redeemed creation with sin, suffering and death utterly obliterated. When our glorification occurs, the groaning creation will be delivered from the bondage to which it was subjected and in its own way, it will share in all that that glory means to us.

The Life That Now Is

I think I know a few people who are so full of life (as full as one can be in this life) that they have little patience with any talk about gloom or trouble or chronic illness. That makes sense to me for what has health in common with disease and what fellowship has vibrant life with clinical depression and despair?

But while I think I understand it I have little sympathy with such a mindset. There's simply too much pain and loss in the world for us go on our merry way with little or no thought for the heartache and the cramped nature of life that others endure for years (compare the selfish approach of Xerxes/Ahaseurus in Esther 4:2). It is no shame—no shame at all—to take pleasure in the blessings God gives us, so to insist on living in a state of misery, prisoners of conscience when God has provided us with every means for present joy is no way to carry on.

But still, there's Matthew 25:31-46 to consider and we are required to live out the difference between glutting ourselves without thought for others and a healthy thanksgiving (note Luke 12:13-21 and 1 Timothy 4:3-4). That may be a tougher job than it appears at first glance but it's what we're called to. E. Stanley Jones quotes a poet unknown to me who wants "to sing lyrics" but goes on to say:

> But how can I sing lyrics?
> I who have seen today
> The stoop of factory women,
> And children kept from play.
> And on an open hilltop,
> Where the cloak of the sky is wide,
> Have seen a tree of terror
> Where a black man died.
> I want to sing lyrics, lyrics,
> But these have hushed my song,
> I am mute at the world's great sadness,
> And stark at the world's great wrong.

The Christ who raged at the injustice and irreverence that went on in the temple (John 2:13-16) and wept over Jerusalem's spiritual state and the coming catastrophe (Matthew 23:37-39 and Luke 19:41-44) would understand very well what the poet meant.

The sheer lack of food and clothing and warmth are the basics but people don't live by bread and clothes and shelter alone. Sustained injustice and the awareness of utter helplessness take their toll and make the world a spinning Alcatraz or a cosmic Belsen. Bad enough that *any* real suffering should exist but people look at one another and wonder why the world situation is so lop-sided. It's clear that, whatever else is true, much of the suffering is in the world because of sin but why should some (tens of millions) bear the lion's share of it? These are serious questions for another time and place but there's no getting away from the world's great sadness and pain and its power to kill hope and generate despair.

Ariel, the wife of the famous agnostic historian, Will Durant, tells us that in his early years Durant had prayed with tears that God might consider letting Lord Byron out of hell because, Durant thought, he had suffered enough. Byron, as you may know, was the brilliant poet who had given himself over to sensuality and who when he was dying didn't think it was right for him to beg for mercy. I can't help thinking that there is something fine about the responses of both men. In any case, Byron wrote a poem (poetry and some history) about Francois de Bonnivard, a prior at a monastery near Geneva, the character in *The Prisoner of Chillon.* As Byron tells it, it is a moving story; three of them chained to pillars, he and his two brothers, the steady loss of hope and the sad death of the two younger men. He tells of Bonnivard's climb to a high window, a look out into blue skies, distant homes and a pretty island where the wind stirred the trees while birds flew free. Now the cell he inhabited had become a coffin more than a cell and we can imagine him for the first time beating on his cell door, choking and sobbing, "Let me out, let me out, dear God I've got to get out of here." After some years when they came to set him free he bore the inner scars of his long imprisonment and he confesses:

> It was at length the same to me,
> Fetter'd or fetterless to be,
> I learn'd to love despair.
>
> .   .   .   .
>
> My very chains and I grew friends,
> So much a long communion tends
> To make us what we are:—even I
> Regain'd my freedom with a sigh.

I wonder if poor Byron in his sensual prison didn't often wish for freedom but found his chains too strong? I wonder did he give up in despair and settle for his awful cell? I know that people can be worn down to the point where even gospel is too good to believe. When Moses brought the gospel to Israel (see Hebrews 4:1-2) we're told "but they would not listen to Moses, because of their broken spirit and their cruel slavery" (Exodus 6:9).

It isn't _just_ the pain and the deprivation and the fact that at this point no one is doing or can do anything to change it. It's the growing conviction that no one _ever will_ or _ever can_ change it. If people were told "seven lean years are coming but after that it'll be paradise" it would make the lean years easier (not easy!) to take but where hope has died so dies the future. To be born in squalor—moral and otherwise—and raised in squalor tends to make us believe that's how we'll die. (Which is why it's _so_ important that we do _something_ to ease the burden of a person in that situation.)

Let me pass by the case of those people whose lives are socially pleasant and morally decent. Part of their temptation is to underestimate their dependence on God and to underestimate how unlike Christ they are despite their decency. Let me address the case of those whose lives are one long moral war, battling to do what is right. To those of us who are like that it is absolutely imperative that we get _the gospel!_ The gospel and nothing less than the gospel! And by the gospel I don't just mean the assurance of forgiveness; I mean the assurance that fullness of life includes holy victory and freedom. There are hosts of us that have never come to Christ because we're sure that he can't possibly want us when we can't even promise to cease our crasser wickedness. And there are hosts of us that came believing he would receive us but were looking for more than forgiveness. We came crippled and imprisoned and we wanted someone to conquer our sins for us; we wanted _life_ and _holy character._ Others might choose to believe the gospel but people like us are so desperate we _must_ believe it because despair hides but it's never far away! We need to be convinced that Christ is the one who can both forgive our sin and drive it out of our lives.

The Life That Could Be Now

I haven't been able to trace where, but somewhere, Bertrand Russell, the British mathematician, agnostic and philosopher, told of a sad reality he was sure he observed. He took notice of apes in a zoo and observed, he thought, that when they were not cracking nuts or doing their gymnastic feats that they had a strange, strained sadness in their eyes. It seemed like to him, Russell said, that these creatures felt left behind, that their human cousins had gone another direction and that they had gone down a dead end. He imagined that they knew there was a way to a higher and better life but they didn't know how to find it.

And then he remarked wistfully that he thought he saw the same strange sadness in the eyes of people when they weren't filling their days with the surface things they do. He thought that like the apes they too were sure there was a way to a higher and better life but they didn't know how to get there. I don't doubt for a moment that millions of people (including Russell) have felt and do now feel precisely that.

And I know it must irritate people for us to say so but Jesus was sure he knew where fullness of life was to be found. He said (John 5:21) that just as surely as the Father gives life "the Son gives life." And with a boldness that offends more than half the world and much of the "Christian world" he said, "I am the way, the truth and the life, nobody comes to the Father but by me" (John 14:6). And without a hint of qualification (though he would want us to qualify it in some way) he claimed that all that came before him were robbers but that he had come that people might have "life, and have it to the full" (John 10:10). And how does that come about? He tells us that it's brought about because he lays down his life for the sheep (10:11).

He said something else. Unless a kernel of wheat falls into the ground and dies it remains alone. But if it dies it bears much fruit. He said that first about himself and then about all those who want life in him (John 12:24-25). I recognize that there is a moral and spiritual principle here that is true for "any person" (12:25) but I don't want to move from the truth that this is first about Jesus Christ who knew that the hour of his death had come (12:23). All this reminds us that life for us begins at and is sustained in the cross of Christ. (You might be interested to see this worked out for Christ's disciples in a little thing I've planned called *In the Steps of the Dragon Slayer.*)

As strange as it might sound, life begins with a long rapturous look at the death of Christ because if anyone has risen to fullness of life it is Jesus Christ and he did it through the cross. *So the cross must be the way to life. His* cross must be the way to *our* life! And it *is* the way to life because in the end the cross is not about death at all. "I have been crucified with Christ, nevertheless I live," Paul said. "Look at me," he seems to say, "wouldn't you think I'd be dead since I have been crucified with Christ? Not a bit of me! I'm alive!" Of Christ he said that he died that those who live might live on a new plane (2 Corinthians 5:15). In 2 Corinthians 4:10-12 he talks about the death of Christ and how it is reenacted in apostolic (and other) lives and the aim and result was what? Life! Listen to what he says there.

> We always carry around in our body the death of Jesus, so that the life of Jesus may also be revealed in our body. For we who are alive are always being given over to death for Jesus' sake, so that his life may be revealed in our mortal body. So then, death is at work in us, but life is at work in you.

Did you notice that? "We who are *alive"* are always being given over to death so that life might be the result. Not just physically alive; alive in that death-defying way in Christ. And in their lives they keep dying, "and see—we are alive" (2 Corinthians 6:9). Ephesians 2:1-10 insists that the life that comes to us through Jesus Christ is *resurrection* life. We gain it not simply because he is alive (a massive truth) but because he is alive *from the dead!* He doesn't offer life that can be torn from us again by death. He gives us the kind of life that is his own, post-death life, death-defeating life and death-destroying life. The life he brings to those who are related to him is deathless life precisely because the sting of death has been destroyed (1 Corinthians 15:56)! And, listen, the life that is ours through Jesus Christ is not just "spiritual" life in the sense that our "souls" are saved—we are saved and not just a part of us. That life we now experience as a relationship with Christ is expressed through our bodies and they were bought by Christ (1 Corinthians 6:20). So even now, it isn't "the soul" of Jennifer or Harry that's saved—it's Jennifer and Harry!

Sin had destroyed the relationship they had with God and so they were dead in their sins (Ephesians 2:1 and Colossians 2:13). That death would soon show itself in the biological death of their bodies. Sin, which brought death in every sense in which that word can be used was defeated in and through Christ. But by faith Harry and Jennifer were united to Jesus Christ who was alive in every possible sense of the word so they too were made alive with him unto God (Colossians 2:13, Romans 6:10-11 and Ephesians 2:4-5). That resurrection life, which is life beyond sin and death, was now theirs and would ultimately show itself in and through the resurrection and glorification of their bodies. Their resurrection was embraced in Christ's resurrection and it would be their final vindication (compare Romans 4:25). This life, in Christ, which is a grand brawl (yes!) and a real adventure gets even better later on.

I think I know people whose lives are one serious wrestle day after day after day. They get tired! They're physically, emotionally and otherwise worn down and nearly worn out. It isn't something that a good eight-hour sleep will cure (though, God knows, if they could get one of those they'd think they were halfway to Paradise). They've tried all the little social and mental tricks to ease the brain. They've read with deep irritation silly books that tell them every problem in life is part of "the small stuff" that they aren't to sweat and they fling them against the wall in justified irritation. Nonsense books like those are written for people whose lives need nothing more than a little fine-tuning to make them heavenly. For the really troubled they're a sharp stick in the eye and a real pain in the heart.

In the movie *As Good As It Gets* Mr. Udhall is a man with serious problems of the compulsive behavioral kind (they are pleasantly made to look funny in the movie). Beneath his rudeness, self-centeredness and sheerly insulting behavior is someone who wishes he was free and at peace like so many others around him. Because of his inner turmoil he resents the harmony in their lives and so, when he can, he makes them pay dearly for their good fortune. This further isolates him and screws the coffin lid down a bit tighter on him.

But he's demented and sometimes his excessive ordering of his ways doesn't help and his pain makes him scream out for help. He bursts into the doctor's office and is promptly told to leave without consultation and as he leaves through the crowded waiting room he looks at the people lining the walls. Their needs are written all over their faces and in their body language as they lounge dispiritedly. He says to them, *"What if this is as good as it gets?"*

Whatever the shortcomings of the movie it is truly worth watching because it images *redemption* for us and if Hollywood can imagine it though without God, shouldn't believers be able to do it with God? For Udhall, things take a lovely turn and a whole new way of living begins. I have no wise pieces of advice for people who live with the screws tightening on their hearts but I have heard Someone say that if we give our lives to him that life as it now is, is *not* as good as it gets! He says he came to give us life to the full and he never lies. (If you'd like to give your life to Christ and you think I might be able to help, contact me, please.)

Let me say it again, Christ's present life is immortal life, life that death can't touch, life that means, for him personally, that death no longer exists. Christ's life is *resurrection* life but only those who have known death can experience resurrection life so clearly he has defeated death. And knowing that that is true of him, belonging to him by faith transforms this world and this life.

You find that hard to believe? Surely not, for you must have experienced world transformation in some form at some time? In his book *Man to Man,* R.E. Welsh describes it.

When the man's love-light is lit by *the one woman,* love reveals to him a new world, and adds another province to his life. What he smiled at as infatuation in other people has become the elixir of his own existence, thrilling him with all the wonder of a new discovery. He had observed it as a pretty element in love-poetry and stories, but now it is dancing in his blood, touching the world with colour and charm, tuning his life to a new motive. The maiden on her part had been callow and variable, with centre everywhere; but at 'The Coming of Love' a flush of warm womanhood mounts into her face; her nature develops, rounds and ripens and blossoms; love gives her a centre and a soul. For each of them this mystical experience is a sort of second birth. It would seem foolish and impossible for them to explain it to you; you must feel it to know it; and it laughs happily at cold common-sense, for it is a new sense.

You think this silly old nonsense? The kind of thing that belongs only to the Mills & Boone type literature? Then hear what Paul said in 2 Corinthians 5:14-17 and think again.

For Christ's love compels us, because we are convinced that one died for all, and therefore all died. And he died for all, that those who live should no longer live for themselves but for him who died for them and was raised again. So from now on we regard no one from a worldly point of view. Though we once regarded Christ in this way, we do so no longer. Therefore, if anyone is in Christ, he is a new creation; the old has gone, the new has come!

From scripture, literature, and life, the word is the same. Find a throbbing center and the world changes. This is true not only in the realm of human love (including romance—I say including because family and friends have the same power) it is true in the realm of the spirit. Ultimately, and at its highest, it is true in relation to the cross. New eyes, new ears, a new spirit and a brand new life begin in union with Christ and because that's true Paul speaks of a "new creation". And this new creation, this new world-view and all that that means rises directly from the cross (5:15 and the "so" or "therefore" in 5:16).

John Masefield's *Everlasting Mercy* tells us of the conversion of Saul Kane and demonstrates with power how the whole world changes once a person lays hold of Jesus (or more fundamentally, is laid hold of by Jesus). Saul Kane was a hard-drinking, blaspheming brawler who had no time for morals and less time for God but he came around like a well-handled ship and the world was never the same.

> I did not think, I did not strive,
> The deep peace burned my me alive;
> The bolted door had broken in,
> I knew that I had done with sin.
>
> .   .   .   .
> O glory of the lighted mind.
> How dead I'd been, how dumb, how blind,
> The station brook, to my new eyes,
> Was babbling out of Paradise;
> The waters rushing from the rain
> Were singing Christ has risen again.
> I thought all earthly creatures knelt
> From rapture of the joy I felt.

But why haven't we all felt it that way? I don't think there's a single answer that covers all cases but isn't part of the answer that we haven't really seen the truth, haven't truly understood the gospel? Some years ago a friend of mine, over a period of about six months, sent me twenty-five or thirty tapes by a famous preacher and author and I listened to every one of them. I tell you in the sight of God that while they were jam-packed with moral exhortation and inspiration there was so little gospel in them I was flabbergasted. It was a ceaseless stream of what we should do, the kind of people we should be and how we can become those people. But about what God had done, what Christ had accomplished and what the Spirit was bringing to the world? Almost nothing! I don't say that that's our sole problem but I am saying we should be ashamed of ourselves if we have substituted even moral exhortation and encouragement for *the gospel!* The gospel is bigger than that and the gospel is more focused than that and if the gospel is not immediately related to moral exhortation then moral exhortation is corrupt and corrupting. It's too easy to become a disciple of the things we need to be and do to be a disciple and to miss the Lord of the disciple.

Be that as it may, those who are Christ's are Christ's! And whatever our struggles, however poorly we appropriate the peace and joy and power in Christ via his Holy Spirit and no matter the reasons why that's the case, if the relationship with Christ is intact *life is ours!* Our feelings and struggles are not a true appraisal of the Holy Father's faithfulness.

Christ's victory over sin is just that—a triumph. Sin is his enemy and ours. He triumphed over it all through his life and he triumphed over it in his atoning death when he neutralized it and rendered it powerless to keep God and his children apart. He conquered it in us as individuals when he turned us from it and turned us to him in saving faith. His triumph brought us forgiveness and inner realignment with the Holy Father, which shows itself in our hunger for his holy fellowship. So maybe we're underestimating what Christ has done in us. Do we think we defeated our sin by ourselves, and turned ourselves to him? Do we think that our humble repentance was the product of our own proud and willful hearts? Do we think that our saving faith is our own creation, self-reflective and self-sustaining? I know (I know!) the moral struggle goes on and bitter disappointment is not uncommon food for us but, praise God, we're alive! Brought back from a death deeper and more putrid than that of Lazarus. And there's more, for the same power that gave us inner life promises to complete that life-giving work in a glorious resurrection to deathless *life*. Here's how the Christ put it in John 5:25,28-29:

> I tell you the truth, a time is coming and has now come when the dead will hear the voice of the Son of God and those who hear will live...Do not be amazed at this, for a time is coming when all who are in their graves will hear his voice and come out—those who have done good will rise to live, and those who have done evil will rise to be condemned.

The reality of the inner life bears witness to the coming of the completed life. In conquering our sin to bring us inner life Jesus conquered that which is the sting of death and brought us under subjection to death (1 Corinthians 15:58 and Romans 5:12-17). So that in defeating sin the Christ proves himself Lord of death (Colossians 1:18b and Revelation 1:18)—resurrection is inevitable!

The Life That Is to Be

The New Testament doctrine of the resurrection is more than the proposal that there is life after death. It's incalculably more than that. Multiplied millions believe in life after death but deny the doctrine of the resurrection. Countless millions want to get rid of the body and in fact, multiplied millions want to get rid of "matter" entirely. C.S. Lewis warned us against becoming more spiritual than God because, he said, God likes matter—he made a lot of it.

Hinduism (and Christian Science) says there is no suffering or death and claims that these are *maya* (illusion) while Buddhism virtually claims there is nothing *but* suffering and death. Buddhism offers life after death but it is not even remotely like the biblical, and specifically New Testament, teaching. On that view life after death is a horror that they wish didn't exist. Their reincarnation doctrine is no doctrine of resurrection; it is part of a horrible cycle these people want to be done with. The heaven they strive for is the utter loss of *individual* existence and with it the destruction of all desire. The lucky one who gains that "heaven" (Nirvana) loses all *individual* consciousness and is absorbed into the cosmos itself; the way a drop of water is absorbed in the ocean. For religions like that the body is *not* for the Lord! It is a burden, and the aim is to get rid of it—eternally rid of it. The Christian faith insists with Paul (1 Corinthians 6:13) that the body is for the Lord and not for fornication *or* the grave. *Part of the meaning of the resurrection of Christ is that God is making good his claim that the body is for him.* But Paul goes on to say something astonishing. "The Lord is for the body." What does that mean? Much Greek thought would despise it and want rid of it (as Hindu/Buddhist thought would) but Christ came and chose it. Brands of asceticism would abuse and revile it but the Lord would honor it. All false "spiritualism" would jettison it and destine it to corruption but the Lord will glorify and immortalize it.

The life that Christ brings is completed in us when he utterly obliterates sin and suffering and death and we find ourselves immortal and in a new and heaven and a new earth wherein dwells only righteousness (compare 1 Peter 1:3-5).

What is now true of Christ personally and individually will finally and completely be true of all those who come to God through him. The present life that is brim full of life will be consummated when we reign with him over a redeemed creation (Romans 8:17-23) with sin and sickness and death things of the past.

Christ was born of a woman and under the torah (Galatians 4:4) and he was son of Adam (Luke 3:23-38 and Matthew 1:1-16). His roots were firmly in human soil since he was made in the likeness of sinful flesh (Romans 8:3), having chosen to take on him our humanity (Hebrews 2:14-18 and Philippians 2:7-8). Like the rest of his sinning human family he was a son of Adam though he was free of the family's sin. But he died not only *in* the flesh he died *to* the flesh and was raised to glory and incorruption. He wasn't made alive again as others (like Lazarus) who remained in the realm of flesh and blood and so subject to death *and all that goes with* being "in Adam" or "in the flesh". No, with Christ and in Christ a new way of being human began that retained humanness but rose beyond the merely fleshly way of existing as a human. Jesus Christ is himself a man (1Timothy 2:5) but his mode of living *as a human* belongs to another "realm" (see 1 Corinthians 15:45-48). Just as we bear the image of the old Adam and are earthy so those embraced in Christ will bear his image—the image of the new and last Adam (1 Corinthians 15:49 and 1 John 3:2). We're not talking about a new way of being *a ghost!* We are humans and remain humans.

Our fleshly bodies (like Adam's) are "natural" bodies (1 Corinthians 15:44). They are designed for living in this realm of "soul life" and aren't suited for the final manifestation of the kingdom of God. They are perishable and belong to this present realm of weakness and vulnerability so they will be transformed (1 Corinthians 15:50-51). Christ's body was also that kind of body while he lived in this realm of weakness (note 2 Corinthians 13:4) and it was in that body of his flesh that he died (1 Peter 3:18—"flesh"). It was in the body of his flesh that he bore our sins (Colossians 1:22 and Ephesians 2:15) because atonement must not only come from above. If it is to mean anything for man it must rise out of humanity—this it did in the person of our representative. It was Christ's mortal body that was glorified in resurrection and transformation so that it is now a "heavenly" or "spiritual" body (compare Philippians 3:20-21).

In 1 Corinthians 15:44 the word behind "natural" is *psuchikon* and the word behind "spiritual" is *pneumatikon.* The adjectives don't describe the "stuff" or substance they're made of but the kind of life, the kind of living they were and are suited for. The "spiritual" body isn't *made of* "spirit" any more than the natural body is *made of* "soul". Our "earthy" body is designed for "soul" life and our "heavenly" bodies are designed for "spiritual" life. Both these are *bodily* life. It isn't that the natural body is a body and the spiritual body *isn't* a body! Paul is speaking of two different forms of *our actual* bodies. This is no abstract, philosophical discussion! Paul is *revealing* and not rationalizing ("behold I show you a mystery"). Both forms of the one body are the work of God and they are empowered by God in different ways for different modes of existence. The life we now experience is "soul" life and our bodies are presently designed to enable us to *be* "living souls" (Genesis 2:7). The life we will later experience as individuals who are part of the risen Christ will be a higher mode of living. And the Spirit that indwells us will enable us to have and express that new experience of life by transforming our present bodies. *But I repeat: both forms of the one body are the work of God and they are empowered in different ways for different modes of existence.* See Romans 8:11, which denies that this body is jettisoned. (N.T. Wright has recently developed this in his massive and marvelous book *The Resurrection of God's Son.)*

And when his personal experience becomes our experience *because* he has experienced it all in our name and for our sake so will end all forms of bondage, subjection, loss, sickness and death. Then the truth of Donne's poem *Death Be Not Proud* will have come home.

> Death, be not proud, though some have called thee
> Mighty and dreadful, for thou art not so;
> For those whom thou thinkst thou dost overthrow
> Die not, poor Death, nor yet canst thou kill me
> *   *   *
> Why swellst thou then?
> One short sleep past, we wake eternally,
> And death shall be no more. Death, thou shalt die.

Some, for their own reasons, insist that our present bodies will be jettisoned. Some say so for reasons that sound suspiciously like the Corinthian protests. Others are afraid that if it is truly *us* who are resurrected we'll pine and be sad over those who "didn't make it" to glory. To avoid that sorrow (since there's to "be no tears in heaven") they have our identity obliterated and we all become strangers. (A radical solution perhaps. One might conjecture that God could easily have made us forget those losses rather than destroy all the wonderful memories that fill us with joy.) But we are more than "bodies". "We" are made of relationships, history, convictions and character forged in fires and joys. To make us faceless wouldn't complete the job. God would have to obliterate everything about us if he is to deal with all sad memories.

Are we to face the loss of all the glorious events and persons that shaped us and made us what we are in Christ? To avoid any sadness are we to forget who God's instruments were to bring us in to the kingdom of his dear Son? Are we to forget the great cost, their holy love and patience? Are we to have no memory of prayers spoken, tears shed and kindnesses done that finally had their way as God stole into the heart he had wooed? All to avoid some sadness that, if necessary at all, could be otherwise obliterated by the gift of partial forgetfulness?

It makes me think of the old Greek story of Charon who was the boatman who took the dead across the River Styx. He reminded a poor woman that she had the right to drink of the Waters of Lethe that would make her forget everything about the life she was leaving. She was keen to drink, saying, "I will forget how I have suffered." Charon told her, "Remember too that you will forget how you rejoiced." She said, "I will forget my failures," and he said, "And your victories as well." She went on, "I'll forget how I was hated" and he reminded her, "You'll forget how you were loved." She thought it over and decided she wouldn't drink.

Our bodies are essentially part of us. We weren't created bodiless spirits and God will redeem the body rather than redeeming us from it. There will be a transformation and glorification of this body but it will be our mortal bodies that are filled with life-filled life (Romans 8:11). "We" will be "we" in the resurrection and we will know one another. All that is worthy of survival will survive on into the life that we will live on a higher plane. But it will be *us* who will live on that higher plane and not a memory-less, experience-less or lobotomized substitute for us. I will not be Ethel's husband then but I will know her and the friendship we shared together in Christ will then be (in actual fact) eternalized. Then my love for her will be free of all those thoughts and attitudes that made our relationship less than it was meant to be "in Christ". The resurrection promises all that. No, *the resurrected Lord* promises all that!

And isn't that good news?

Death in scripture has more than one face. It isn't only God's righteous judgement on sin (Romans 1:32) it's also closely associated with sin which Paul says is death's sting (1 Corinthians 15:56) and so death is seen as an enemy of life with God (15:26,54-55). Biological death is more than the loss of physical life; it's a sign of something more terrifying; it's a sign of humanity's moral and spiritual estrangement from God. The teeming millions that are put away out of our sight, the terminal wards and the mass graves in far-flung countries all scream forth the presence and power of sin in the human family.

Is there any saving of us? With these harsh realities ceaselessly battering our senses is it any wonder whole nations and tribes are locked into nothing more than making it through another day? But there is a Savior! And the hope he gives is not born out of any mere sunny optimism. It is the living hope offered by someone who knows the world as it truly is and has overcome it. Saying no to its seductions and sadness, saying no to its squalor and narrowness, saying no to death and despair he comes alive from the dead to say, "I can save you!"

I love the way he took it on himself to save the unsaveable and to heal the unhealable. When expert opinion, buttressed by rolling centuries of human failure, was certain that we were a lost cause he came, rolled up his sleeves and went to work. And I think what pleases me is that he did so much of his costly healing and saving work while we were oblivious to it.

In Maclaren's novel *Beside The Bonnie Brier Bush,* Lord Kilspindie's famous London doctor looked in on Saunders and said he couldn't live more than three or four hours, much less through the night. Saunders's wife Bell was beside herself and while waiting for local doctor MacLure she sobbed her heart out to Drumsheugh, a close family friend. When the old man arrived he confirmed the big city doctor's word that the man was terribly ill and under threat of death. Bell was sure she already saw the shadow of death that never lifts lying plainly on the man she adored and needed; but after examining the man he had known since childhood, MacLure insisted, "It's hoverin, Bell, but it hesna fallen."

"Do you think, Willum, he has a chance?" whispered Drumsheugh. "That he hes, at ony rate, and it'll no' be your blame or mine if he hesna mair," growled the old man, taking off his coat and rolling up his sleeves. And with the London doctor's viewpoint in mind, he said, "It's maybe presumptuous o' me tae differ frae him, and it wudna be verra respectfu' o' Saunders tae live aifter this opeenion."

Drumsheugh later said it made his blood race all the way to his fingertips to see old MacLure's bracing himself for the battle. "For a' saw noo there was tae to be a stand-up fecht atween him an' deith for Saunders."

The distraught and worn-out wife was sent to bed and he and Drumsheugh prepared for a no-holds barred brawl with the intruder. The fever raged and the disease attacked but MacLure dabbed and bathed, massaged and prayed, thumped and turned his patient, listened intently and then quietly barked out orders to Drumsheugh to get or do this or that. Through the long night, promising nothing but giving no quarter, MacLure, with iron face, fought for the life of a man who knew nothing of all that was being done to and for him. A bundle of jerking skin and bones that rasped with every tortured breath he took, was lifted and laid back down by a big old doctor who was as gentle as a woman with a baby; often on his knees as he worked beside the low cot on which Saunders lay.

Weary himself from the heat and tension of it all and hearing the old man say they were holding their own, Drumsheugh went into the darkness of the surrounding fields for a breath of fresh air while MacLure continued his ceaseless vigil for every sound or change in temperature or appearance. It was the hour before daybreak and he could just make out the forms of the sleeping cattle. Sitting down he could hear the gurgling talk of the distant stream as it made its way over the stones. An owl hooted, startling him and reminding him of a childhood fright when he ran home to his mother; now a long time dead. He looked at the shadow of his own dark, cold house on the hill, a place with no loved one in it and then back to Saunders's lighted house where love was sleeping in hope and where love was fighting in earnest self-giving for the life of the man. Lonely himself and weary with the wrestle, an indescribable sadness came over him; how futile and mysterious this life was.

But in the middle of all this weariness he sensed a subtle change in the night, and the air around him seemed to tremble as if somebody had whispered. He lifted his head eastward and the grey of a cloud slowly reddened before his watching eyes. The sun wasn't yet on the horizon but it was on its way; and the cattle stirred, rose and stretched, a blackbird, uninvited, burst into the first song of the morning and as Drumsheugh crossed Saunders's doorstep the sun was just showing itself above a peak of the Grampians.

The look on the doctor's face said things were going well for the sick man. MacLure said, "It's ower sune to say mair, but a'm houpin' for the best." Drumsheugh leaned back in a chair to rest and before he dozed off he saw the old man sitting erect in his chair, a clenched fist resting on the bed and eyes bright with the vision of triumph in them. He awoke with a start to find the room flooded with sunshine and all evidence of the night's battle gone. The doctor was leaning over the bed, talking to Saunders, and giving him a sip of milk and telling him to go asleep again. The patient went into a deep, healthy slumber.

The old man put on his vest and jacket and went out into the sunlit air and Drumsheugh followed him without a word. Out they went through the dewy garden, past Saunders's corn that was ready for the scythe and into an open field. Suddenly the doctor dragged off his coat and threw it west; his vest went east and he began shaking and jumping. As he danced in unrestrained delight he was shouting, "Saunders wesna to live through the nicht, but he's livin' this meenut, an' like to live...It'll be a graund waukenin' for Bell; she 'ill no' be a weedow yet, nor the bairnies fatherless."

And then, as though Drumsheugh's look was rebuking him, he said, "There's nae use glowerin' at me, Drumsheugh, for a body's daft at a time, an a' canna contain masel', and a'm no' gaein' tae try." It was then that his friend realized the old man was attempting the Highland fling. Later, talking to his friends about the whole matter, Drumsheugh confessed, "A' hevna shaken ma ain legs for thirty years, but a' confess tae a turn masel'...the thought o' Bell an' the news that wes waitin' her got the better o' me."

And so the two friends, shaped by their age and a community's reserve in expressing itself, threw off the restraints of custom and in the face of a glorious triumph danced and laughed their way home on a glorious morning.

The word spread throughout Drumtochty and nothing else was talked about when the glen was gathered outside the church that following Sunday morning. Just at that time they saw the doctor approaching on his horse. If only it wasn't Sunday; what a cheer they would send up. As the old man got nearer the pent up feelings grew stronger. If only it wasn't "the Sabbath". As he came up to the crowd up went a cheer of "Hurrah!" and "Hurrah again!" and a hat was seen waving on the other side of the church wall. It was the minister's—of all people! The doctor's horse couldn't bear it and carried him off in a canter while the conservative Drumtochty glen regained its decorum. But not without a lingering satisfaction.

Isn't that a great story? But the biblical Story goes way beyond that. The Dragon Slayer offers more than simple life from the dead or the continuation of life as we now experience it; he offers *resurrection* life. The destruction of death promised in 1 Corinthians 15:25-26 is a complete obliteration of death by the introduction of glorious and deathless life! Adam and the risen, glorified Christ ("the last Adam") are not just two individuals; they represent two modes of living. Those merely united to Adam experience only "soul" life in a "natural" (soul) body but those who are united to the living Christ now live life that is life beyond sin, life that exists not because of "breath" or any other "natural" power source. And one day they will fully experience that resurrection life as their representative now fully experiences it. Their bodies will undergo a transformation and be made like his own glorious body (Philippians 3:20-21 and Romans 8:10-11).

The guarantee of our glorious resurrection is the Christ's! He is the "firstfruits" (1 Corinthians 15:23) which says that the whole harvest is on its way. In the Old Testament the firstfruits represents the whole crop or the whole flock (in the case of sheep, for example). In offering the best of the first ones to arrive, the worshiper confesses that the whole belongs to God and by offering that portion the whole is dedicated to God. Representation is a central element in this as it is in all other offerings. (A tithe confesses all their prosperity belongs to and comes from God; a day confesses the same about all days, etc.)

It's while reflecting on things like these that the ordinances of baptism and the Lord's Supper really come home to us. William Willimon from Duke preached a grand lesson he called *Don't Forget Your Baptism* in which he connected these vital gospel truths to the ordinance. Neville Clark from Oxford in his *Interpreting the Resurrection* offers this, "It is in baptism that the Resurrection reality is ever and anew proclaimed. Here the Easter event is made contemporary and visible. Here the earth trembles, and the stone is rolled away, as the power of the new age moves decisively forward in the work of re-creation. For the baptized man has put on Christ, has been re-clothed in his risen life, has been drawn across the chasm and given the freedom of the new world." (I confess that when I was being baptized into the Christ I didn't see it in such a glorious way. Praise God for his inexpressible grace and mercy and generosity!)

And the church (the body of Christ) lives only in the power of the resurrection. His resurrection was the beginning of the "new creation" (compare 2 Corinthians 5:17) and his final coming will be the consummation of it. So on each new "Lord's" day when we eat the bread and drink the wine (as "one loaf" and "one body"—1 Corinthians 10:16-17) we become *announcers* (not whisperers or mutterers) of the Lord's death "until he comes" (1 Corinthians 11:26).

O precious Lord Jesus who heard that we were sick unto death and refused to believe that we were beyond healing; who labored and sweated over us with such self-denying as no mortal has ever known and who, when we were returned safe and sound from the clutches of death by your own selfless work, rejoiced and were glad beyond our knowing because we were rescued. Thank you for doing for us things we didn't know you were doing and doing them without waiting for us to ask your help. For all this and more we are thankful beyond our ability to tell, though we know we are not thankful enough. Take our sinner's gratitude and let it be only an acknowledgement of and not the repayment for what we owe you. Thank you for wrestling in the dark with the baleful and brutal intruder so that we wouldn't sink without trace and thank you that you find us precious enough to rejoice over.

And because of who you are and what you have done, because you feel about us as you do, we commit ourselves to your service and your keeping with full assurance and gladness of heart. And how pleased we are to know that the day is coming when that resurrection life you now experience and keep in trust for us will be our own actual experience and we will serve you eternally and better then than now. Amen.

God's Creation Purposes

It was from the cross that Jesus rose to glory and Lordship and I want to suggest that Christ's resurrection is immediately linked to the glorification of the entire creation and that that glorification had always been a part of God's eternal purpose. I want to suggest that the life God blessed us with originally was glorious, but mortal, and that he purposed to bring us from that to glorious life beyond mortality. The Dragon who brought us sin brought us death and God through the Dragon Slayer brought us life beyond sin and death. This connects atonement and redemption with God's creation purposes. All this and more the resurrection of Christ means and includes. (The Old Testament is permeated with the truth that creation and redemption are seen as the work of the one true God. See Psalm 136 as a single illustration of this and then look for more.)

In six days, we're told, God created and on the seventh day he rested. This isn't the place to offer suggestions on what that Sabbath rest means but it's clear that some kind of completion is implied though we aren't to make that completion absolute since Christ said otherwise (John 5:16-17). Taking our cue from 1 Corinthians 15:45-49, Romans 5:14, Colossians 1:16 and the summary of Romans 8:30 it appears that God always intended to bring his creation (humanity included) to greater glory than it originally had.

When we chose sin and rebellion against our sovereign Lord we dragged creation down with us and God brought the curse down on it as well as on us (see Genesis 3:17-19; 5:29

and compare Romans 8:20). Creation's loss of glory reflected our loss of glory as it refuses to give to its lord his due (Genesis 1:26 and 3:17-19) as we refused to give to our Lord his due.

Israel, as Abraham's children, inherited Canaan's land and that relationship recapitulated the Adam/Eve and earth relationship. Their sin polluted the land, they were vomited out and the land suffered (compare Ezekiel 36:1-21 which is addressed to the land and not the people and then 36:22-38). Israel and Canaan, while historical realities with their own peculiar covenant connections are models of the larger purpose of God and were never intended to be permanently "exclusive". Abraham's children include more than Israel and Canaan is only a shadow of the world (see Romans 4:13-17 and especially 4:13 that tells us Abraham's children were to be heirs of the world). Note Hebrews 4 where the writer speaks of four Sabbaths, one of which is Canaan rest.

On the post-Christ side of sin and the curse, humanity and the rest of creation would enter into glory that transcended the original (see Romans 8:18-23). If this is true it only adds to other material that teaches us that the resurrection of Christ has a significance that goes beyond our own individual hope of glorious resurrection. Christ's resurrection has immediate ramifications for the entire creation (note again Ephesians 1:10 and Colossians 1:20 where all things in heaven and earth are "reconciled" to God). If Christ has been raised then a new Lord of creation (a new Adam) has arrived and a new creation has begun. Since he did it in our name and for our sake we presently share *by faith in Christ* (note 1 Corinthians 3:21-23) what we will share in fact *with* (and because of) Christ (Romans 8:17).

But if God is to fulfil his creation purposes they will have to be fulfilled to a creation that is in fellowship with him because he can't glorify a creation that holds him in contempt and is alien to him. So the work of atonement and reconciliation must take place. But since the eternal purpose was to bring us to glory and immortality then the atonement furthers that purpose. This means that Christ's resurrection to glory and immortality, whatever else it is, is God confirming and fulfilling those creation purposes so that redemption reaffirms creation). Note how Romans 8:30 summarizes (as if it had already been completed) all that chapter 8 has been speaking about and promising.

The resurrection of Jesus is the resurrection of a historical person, of course, but it's more than that. When Paul gasped about what God had done (see Ephesians 1:16-20) in raising Jesus from the dead, he wasn't saying God must have been powerful if he could raise Jesus. He was carried away by the grandeur of what it *meant* that God had raised him. Everybody knew God could raise a dead man—that was no big feat (see Isaiah 40 for a description of power) but what everyone didn't know and what made Paul gasp was what happened when God raised *that* man from the dead to immortality. A whole new creation had begun of which Christ is the source and the church is a part! A new Adam had arrived and a new humanity had begun in him and would flow from him (1 Corinthians 15:48 and Romans 5:14b). A new creation had begun over which the new Adam was given sovereignty (Hebrews 2:5-9 and see Colossians 1:15 which echoes Genesis 1:26-27). That new Adam who was now head over all things in heaven and on earth (Ephesians 1:10) stood for all those that came from him and in him they became heirs (1:11 and Colossians 1:12-13). *That* was what Paul was astonished at and wanted the Ephesians to see. *That* was what God was working out in and through them as being bound up in Christ's resurrection (1:18-21). And we can be sure that the resurrection of Jesus of Nazareth confirms all this because his resurrection points him out as God's unique Son and confirms his place as Lord (Romans 1:4; Philippians 2:9-11 and Acts 2:29-36).

With a new Adam and his fellow-heirs comes a world that has groaned for deliverance and will be delivered when the children of God are finally revealed in all their glory. They'll look like their Lord (see Philippians 3:20-21; Colossians 3:1-4 and 1 John 3:1-2) and they'll reign with him over a redeemed creation (Romans 8:17, and see numerous Old Testament sections that speak of this renewal of Eden and the destruction of wilderness—Isaiah 11 and 35 would illustrate). Sin finally obliterated, death obliterated, the curse removed since it had done well its job and is needed no more. Life abundant!

Some Suggestions for Reading

If you're a patient student and are willing to invest the time I don't know that you could do any better than read P.T. Forsyth. It's true I suppose that he's an acquired taste and at times he's like fireworks in the fog but he's the richest writer I know on the cross. He has numerous volumes that all work around the same theme. *The Centrality of the Cross, The Holy Father, The Justification of God* all of which are smaller books but serious reads. I found his publication *Work of Christ* to be fairly straightforward (they were published lectures) and then there is his *Person And Place of Jesus Christ* which was his major work.

Vincent Taylor has three earlier books all relating to this area. Two of them I found especially helpful, *The Atonement in New Testament Teaching* and *Forgiveness and Reconciliation.* He helped me most by his insistence (without expressing it in these terms) that reconciliation, while it is grounded in Christ's finished work at the cross, is only effectual in the individual when it is internalized. There's nothing unusual in this from the point of view from the Reformers but the way some evangelicals talk in the past forty or fifty years you'd think reconciliation and salvation was a "done deal" apart from saving faith. So anxious are these people to give God all the glory they seem to forget that God is glorified in the saving faith he generates that lays hold of the work completed on the cross. And when many of them do speak about "faith" it is so watered down, so carefully defined that it's more like vapor than faith. It is reduced to a mental confession of the truth that we can't save ourselves. This reductionism isn't helpful or true.

The books of James Denney are still truly valuable. *The Death of Christ* and *The Christian Doctrine of Reconciliation* both stress the objective nature of the atonement though it appears Denney began to say more about the subjective side of it all.

This was no bad thing. He insisted that there is something *in God* that required the atonement and that Jesus' death in some *real* sense made a difference to how God relates to us.

Joel Green and Mark Baker's *Recovering the Scandal of the Cross* is really helpful especially in opening our eyes to the New Testament's use of metaphors in relation to the atoning work of Christ. But it appears to me that the wrath of God vanishes when Green and Baker are done. That's too bad. Still it's a robust and effective challenge to the usual penal substitution view of evangelicalism.

The style of J. Macleod Campbell makes his book a hard read but his *Nature of the Atonement* is an absolute jewel and worth the effort. I'm sure he needs Forsyth and others to balance him but I was really lifted and enlightened by Campbell.

Leon Morris has his excellent (but maybe lop-sided) *Apostolic Preaching & The Cross* and Alister McGrath has an excellent little book in *The Enigma of the Cross.* Most of the later ones I've managed to read are pretty much a rehearsal of what has gone before. Colin Gunton did a very useful work called *The Actuality of Atonement* that deals with the work of Christ under three major headings (justice, victory and sacrifice) as well as introducing us to the use of metaphors in relation to Christ's work. There are literally dozens of older books on the cross and the atonement that are very good but the above come to mind as outstanding (at least to me).

There has been a growing stream of useful material on God's righteousness as faithfulness since Herman Cremer opened our eyes to that truth. Paul Achtmeier has a simple rehearsal of the facts in the *Interpreter's Bible Dictionary* and since then, people like James Dunn (of Durham) and N.T. Wright have been developing it for us (and see Gunton's helpful section on this).

Questions for Personal and Group Reflection

1. How do you know the cross was central to the apostolic faith?
2. Why did the creation need to be reconciled to God?
3. What is "the righteousness of God"?
4. Was God angry with Christ while he was on the cross?
5. Did God punish Christ on the cross?
6. What's the difference between suffering and punishment?
7. How did Heinrich Heine describe the power of the cross?
8. How many crucifixions does Paul see in Galatians 6:14?
9. Does God forbid that the innocent be punished for the sins of the guilty?
10. Has death been abolished?
11. Did Christ conquer the powers at the cross?
12. If he did, why are they alive and well today?
13. What is a "God-man"?
14. Was Jesus a "God-man"?
15. Did Christ have divine genes or blood?
16. Was Jesus an angel being a man?
17. Was Jesus the highest ranked creature being a man?
18. What difference does it make?
19. Why is it important that Jesus was God being a man?
20. Why is it important that Jesus was God being only a man like any other man?
21. What does it mean that Christ "bore" our sins?
22. Did Christ become a sinner on the cross?
23. 2 Corinthians 5:21 says he became "sin"—what exactly does that mean?
24. Are people fed up with doctrine?
25. If they are, why is that a bad thing?
26. What's wrong with summing up the Christian faith as "a fine way to live"?
27. What's right with the poem that begins, "I'd rather see a sermon than hear one any day"?
28. When we approach scripture, what's right with the question, "What does this verse mean to me?"?

29. If the Devil dropped dead at this moment would sinning still continue?
30. What did Karl Barth say God was not willing to be?
31. Why can't God offer an "immoral" forgiveness?
32. What kind of forgiveness might that be?
33. Is God obsessed with sin or with life?
34. Is forgiving sin God's ultimate aim? If not, why not?
35. Is an individual's sin atoned for if her or she rejects God?
36. The writer claims sanctification is reconciliation (one face of it), what does he mean?
37. What does it mean that Christ was made in the likeness of sinful flesh (Romans 8:3)?
38. Philippians 2 said Christ "emptied" himself, why can it not mean that he left behind something that was essential to Godhood?
39. What is "the world" that Christ conquered? Is it an imaginary thing? Is it the planet? The people of the planet? What is it?
40. How did he overcome it? By the fact that he was God? By miraculous power? How is sin overcome?
41. Is Satan the god of the world? What does that mean exactly? Does he rule the world? Does God rule the world?